D1393295

NATURAL ENVIRONMENT RESEARCH COUNCIL
INSTITUTE OF GEOLOGICAL SCIENCES

British Regional Geology

# The Grampian Highlands

(THIRD EDITION)

By G. S. Johnstone, B.Sc.

*Based on previous editions by*
H. H. Read, D.Sc., A.R.C.S., F.R.S.
and A. G. MacGregor, M.C., D.Sc.

EDINBURGH
HER MAJESTY'S STATIONERY OFFICE
1966

*The Institute of Geological Sciences*
*was formed by the*
*incorporation of the Geological Survey of Great Britain*
*and the Museum of Practical Geology*
*with Overseas Geological Surveys*
*and is a constituent body of the*
*Natural Environment Research Council*

*First Published* 1935
*Second Edition* 1948
*Third Edition* 1966
*Reprinted with Amendments* 1973

SBN 11 880155 4

# FOREWORD TO THIRD EDITION

The compilation of a handbook to the Grampian Highlands is a task of considerable complexity because of the wide field of geological subjects it has to cover and the fact that, as research workers are still very active in the area, opinions are constantly being modified. While a large measure of agreement has been reached concerning major problems which, at the time of the 2nd Edition, were still hotly debated, controversy in detail is by no means at an end and it is impossible to present in a handbook of this nature more than a selection of the views held. This is especially the case with the several chapters concerning the Grampian Caledonides and with that dealing with Caledonian Magmatism, which have been considerably generalized in order to provide a synthesis adapted to the needs of the general reader: advanced students are referred for detail and argument to the bibliographies appended.

The view has been taken that many of the diagrams should be sketch maps, constructed to assist the understanding of difficult points in the text, and since in such cases considerable simplifications of the geology have necessarily been made, they should not be regarded as substitutes for the published geological maps as a means of tracing outcrops on the ground. A list of published maps is given at the end of Chapter 2, but the reader will find that the one on the scale of about 10 miles-to-one-inch may suffice for general purposes.

The handbook is based to a great extent on previous editions by Drs. H. H. Read and A. G. MacGregor. Dr. J. D. Peacock has supplied notes incorporated in the sections dealing with the Old Red Sandstone, the Permian, Triassic and Jurassic and the Pleistocene. Dr. T. E. Smith compiled the General Bibliography, while Dr. N. G. Berridge assisted with the compilation of the chapter on Economic Minerals.

---

*An EXHIBIT illustrating the Geology and Scenery of the district described in this volume is set out on the first gallery of the Museum of Practical Geology, Exhibition Road, South Kensington, London, S.W.7.*

# CONTENTS

# FIGURES IN TEXT

# PLATES

# EXPLANATION OF PLATES

*Frontispiece*. Ben Nevis from the Great Glen. The precipice and topmost part of the mountain (centre of view) are formed from lavas of Lower Old Red Sandstone age. The peak on the left and the rounded hill to the right are made of granite of the pluton into which these lavas have foundered. Coire a'Mhuilinn, below the precipice shows the U-shaped form of a well-glaciated valley and 'hangs' above the Great Glen. *View from Muirshearlich, Banavie, Inverness-shire*. D 745.

**Plate**

I The South-west Grampians. Mountains formed by the erosion of a former peneplain, as indicated by the general accordance of summit levels. The rocks comprise Dalradian schists and Caledonian plutonic igneous complexes. *View eastwards to Ben Nevis and the Mamore hills from above Locheilside, Inverness-shire*. D 746.

II A. Mountains formed from schistose grit. The illustration shows the characteristic craggy topography found in much of the area made up from the schistose grits of the Dalradian Upper Psammitic Group. The gently undulating foliation of the rocks within the 'Flat Belt' can be made out. Moundy morainic deposits mantle the lower slopes. *Beinn Chabair, from Glen Falloch, Perthshire*. D 667.
B. Ben Lawers and Loch Tay. Much of the agricultural land on the far shore is made of Loch Tay limestone, with overlying crags of Ben Lui Schists. Ben Lawers Schists on the upper slopes. Strike-line featuring is prominent as the rocks leave the 'Flat Belt' to dip into the Ben Lawers Synform. *View from near Killin, Perthshire*. D 747.

III A. Current-bedding in quartzite. 'Way up' of a cross-bedded unit can be made out by the sharp truncation of the false-bedding (near the hammer head) marking the top and contrasting with the smooth curve of the 'bottomset' beds at the base. (see Plate XIA.) *Glen Coe Quartzite, Glen Nevis, Inverness-shire*. D 748.
B. Folding and cleavage in schistose rocks. The lithological banding is folded into fairly open, sharp-crested folds. Associated with these is a strong, vertical cleavage parallel to the axial planes and imparting a new schistosity to the rocks. *Boulder, probably of Dalradian schists, in the Allt na Lairig, near Lochtreighead, Inverness-shire*. C 1850.

IV A. Large scale folding of Dalradian rocks. Huge folds (probably of Late Caledonoid age) in the Glen Coe Quartzite. Binnein Schists form the smooth ground to the left. The height of section is about 2800 ft. *Sgurr a'Mhaim, Glen Nevis, Inverness-shire*. C 1762.

IV B. *Loch Leven and the Mamore Hills.* Loch Leven is a fiord-like loch eroded along the line of a shatter belt. The hills are formed mainly of Dalradian schists within the Kinlochleven Recumbent Anticline. Ballachulish Slates in the quarry in the foreground (see Plate XIB). *View eastwards from Beinn a' Bheithir, Ballachulish, Argyllshire.* D 749.

V Sketch map of the structures making up the Southern Grampians Nappe-Complex.

VI The Lithological Divisions of the Moinian and Dalradian Rocks of the Grampian Highlands; unornamented land areas comprise Lewisian and Torridonian strata (see Fig. 2), metamorphosed intrusions, and post-Dalradian sediments and igneous rocks.

VII A. Flaggy Moinian granulite. Psammitic (quartzo-feldspathic) granulite with the flaggy aspect typical of much of the Central Highland Granulites. *River Lyon, near Gualann, Perthshire.* C 2296.
B. Contorted Dalradian schist. Schists with alternating micaceous and quartzo-feldspathic laminae, showing intense small-scale folding. *Dalradian Upper Psammitic Group, near Coylet Inn, Loch Eck, Argyllshire.* C 802.

VIII A. The Glen Coe Cauldron-subsidence. The hills on the left and right of the photograph are made of Dalradian schists. The crags in the centre and the distant peaks are formed of lavas of Lower Old Red Sandstone age, downfaulted in a cauldron-subsidence (see Plate VIIIB, below). *Glen Coe, Argyllshire, from Callert on Loch Leven.* D 750.
B. The Glen Coe Boundary Fault. The fault forms the deep gully on the hill on the right. To the right of the fault is granite of the fault intrusion. To the left, phyllites, forming the crags in the foreground, are overlain by Lower Old Red Sandstone volcanic rocks, both being downfaulted in a cauldron-subsidence. The latter rocks also form the peaks in the corrie. *Coire nam Beith from Loch Auchtriochtan, Glen Coe, Argyllshire.* B 619.

IX A. Triassic Sandstone. Sea cliff and stack of false-bedded yellow Triassic Sandstone, both of which have a capping of boulder clay. *Shore at Covesea, near Lossiemouth, Morayshire.* C 1474.
B. Dolerite dykes of the Tertiary swarm. The resistant igneous rocks form stacks, rising from the post-glacial raised beach which has been cut in more easily eroded quartzite. *Near the Allt Bun an Eas, south of Loch Tarbert, Isle of Jura.* C 1244.

X A. Raised Beach. A platform of marine erosion backed by former sea-cliffs. The beach illustrated is one of those thought by W. B. Wright to be pre-glacial (see Chapter 14). *North coast of Islay.* B 725.
B. The Parallel Roads of Glen Roy. Strand-lines on the hillside mark the successive levels of an intermittently-diminishing glacially-impounded lake. *Glen Roy, Inverness-shire.* C 4114.

XI A. *Fluvio-glacial deposits.* False-bedded fluvio-glacial sands infilling a former glacier lake. Topset beds removed by erosion during the formation of a later river terrace. *Spean Bridge, Inverness-shire.* C 4144.

B. *The Ballachulish Slate Quarries.* Abandoned workings in the Ballachulish Slates, showing the typical cleavage of the group and the method of working, in benches. *Ballachulish, Argyllshire.* D 668.

---

*Serial numbers indicate a photograph from the collection of the Geological Survey, taken by the Geological Survey photographic staff: the originals of Plates I, IIB, IIIA, IVB, VIIIA and the Frontispiece were taken by the author.*

# I. INTRODUCTION

## Boundaries of the Area

The boundaries of the region to be described in this handbook are clearly defined by natural topographical features. On the north, the limit is the great trench of Gleann Mor na h-Albain (The Great Glen of Scotland) while on the south, the margin is set by the Highland Border, a line, running from Stonehaven on the north-east to Arran on the south-west, along which the lowlands of the Midland Valley of Scotland abruptly give place northwards to the more rugged and elevated hills of the Scottish Highlands. Both these topographic features follow the lines of faults of major structural importance— the Great Glen and the Highland Boundary (or Border) faults respectively. The area to be described is thus clearly determined both topographically and geologically (Fig. 1).

The name 'Grampian Highlands' has been applied to the greater part of the region and is traditionally supposed to date at least from the time of the Roman Invasion of Britain, for an important battle was fought in A.D. 86 at 'Mons Graupius', possibly in the south-eastern foothills of the region. The question as to whether there is any connection between the words 'Graupius' and 'Grampian' is one for the philologist. In Blaeu's 'Atlas' (1662) a reference is made to 'Grampios Montes' (Alexander 1950), showing that the name was in current use by that time.

## Physical Features

Although the region described in this handbook is by no means all mountainous (Fig. 1) the Grampians proper comprise the highest land in Britain. Ben Nevis reaches 4406 ft O.D. and a considerable area in the Cairngorms exceeds 3500 ft above sea-level. Many of the summits of the remainder of the mountainous area reach or exceed 3000 ft. Viewed from a distance, or from any commanding height within them, the Grampians show a general tendency for the ridges and mountain tops to reach up to a more or less uniform level (Plate I) and the mountains have evidently been carved by the agents of denudation from a former peneplain. The origin of this peneplain has been much discussed, notably by Geikie, Mackinder, Peach and Horne, Bremner, Linton and George and the reader is referred to the list of works by these authors given in the References at the end of this chapter. The peneplain consisted of the worn down remnants of the ancient mountains of the 'Grampian Caledonides' (see Ch. 2) together with their mantle of later strata and George (1955, 1960), in agreement with certain of the earlier investigators, suggested a date of planation and uplift later than the period of Tertiary igneous activity, i.e. Miocene-Pliocene. He pointed out, in addition, that the surface is benched at several levels, indicating pulsatory uplift. Linton (1951), while proposing a date of planation which George showed to be untenable, has also suggested that the maximum elevation of the Highland Peneplain

1

may be in the Ben Nevis–Cairngorm area and that the surface was arched so that there is a general decline in present-day summit levels towards the east and south-east. This would agree with the opinion, advanced by Cadell (1886, 1913), Mackinder, and Peach and Horne, that the original drainage of the Highlands developed on an easterly-tilted surface and that consequent rivers thus flowed in a generally easterly direction. Relics of these ancient river valleys are thought to be represented in the south-west Grampians by the valleys of Glen Nevis, the Lairigmor (with its continuation valley to the east of Loch Leven) and Glen Coe (Geological Survey memoir 'Ben Nevis and Glen Coe', Fig. 1). In the southern part of the area the Loch Sloy and Loch Katrine valleys probably mark the line of the ancestor of the River Forth, while the Garry–Tay is the chief consequent river of the central part of the Grampians.

As the overlying Old Red Sandstone and later rocks were denuded off the Highland peneplain, the metamorphic rocks of the Grampian Caledonides were revealed. These consist of rocks of varied resistance to erosive agents, and form belts running in a general north-north-east to south-south-west direction. Continued denudation led to the formation of longitudinal streams running in valleys carved out of the weaker members of the metamorphic rocks, or controlled by the strike-directions of these. The River Spey, an example of these longitudinal streams, seems to have cut back so as to intercept the old consequent streams of the North-west Highlands as far west as Loch Eil. Again, the development of an active longitudinal tributary of the Garry–Tay along a belt of weak strata and shattered rocks in the present Loch Tay district led to the relegation of the consequent Garry to a minor position. The continued adjustment of the river-system as the heterogeneous foundation of crystalline rocks was eroded more and more has led to departures from the simple consequent or longitudinal character of individual streams, whilst capture of portions of one river-system by another has occurred in many districts. As examples of this last process may be instanced the capture of the headwaters of the River Dee (the Geldie Burn) by the Feshie, and of the Upper Don by the Avon.

In addition to the factors already noted, the denudation of the Grampian Highlands has been markedly influenced by a group of faults, with accompanying belts of shattered and weakened rocks, which run in a general north-north-easterly, or northerly, direction. Although these shatter-belts cross many great valleys without affecting their courses, they have been seized upon in many cases by the agents of denudation and deep hollows formed along them. They are particularly well developed in the South-west Highlands (see Ch. 15 and Fig. 21).

The plain on the south side of the Moray Firth, and its continuation in the Buchan promontory of Aberdeenshire, are partly due to the removal of a series of soft Mesozoic and Old Red Sandstone strata from the underlying platform of metamorphic and igneous rocks on which the former previously rested with unconformity.

The lochs of the Central Highlands have a remarkable distribution. Apart from the small examples in the high corries of the Cairngorms, only a few are found north-east of a line drawn from Inverness to Perth. South-west of this line occur the grandest lochs of the Highlands. As Peach and Horne pointed out, this contrast depends fundamentally upon the difference in the character of the Highland peneplain in the two regions at the beginning of the Glacial Period. In the first region (Fig. 1) there were extensive areas of poorly-dissected peneplain, the valleys were open and comparatively shallow and led gradually up to high ground. No concentration of ice-erosion was possible. The second region, on the other hand, is a highly dissected district where deep through-valleys have been established between high mountains, and where the cols form low passes across the existing watershed. In such regions ice-reservoirs were established and, from these, vast quantities of ice passed out by somewhat restricted outlets. As an example of such a cauldron may be given the Moor of Rannoch, from which lead the outlets now containing Loch Rannoch, Loch Ericht, Loch Treig, etc. (see Ch. 14). It will be seen

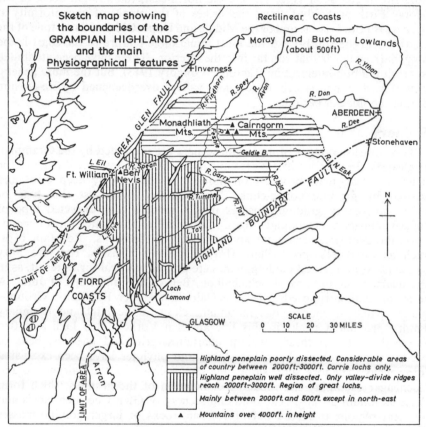

FIG. 1. *Physiography of the Grampian Highlands*
For additional names of major lochs see Figs. 4 and 5, also Plate V

from the foregoing, therefore, that the lochs of the South-western Highlands can be explained as due to glacial erosion. The work of the Scottish Loch Survey under Sir J. Murray and L. Pullar showed that the great lochs occupying rock-basins possessed features readily explicable by ice-erosion. Such features are: U-shape in cross-section, lack of adjustment between the large valley rock-basins and tributary streams, the presence of several distinct basins in one loch, and the occurrence of the greatest depths where the valley is most constricted and of the steepest slopes at concave bends where ice-erosion was most powerful. In some cases, the original hollow coincided with a belt of shattered rock along which erosion was exceedingly active. For instance, Loch Ericht, lying along such a shatter-belt, has a length of fourteen and a half miles but a width not exceeding half a mile, whilst its greatest depth, 512 ft, occurs at the constricted part of the loch. As a typical valley rock-basin may be instanced Loch Lomond, which lies across the strike of the strata in a valley in great part excavated by one of the original consequent streams draining towards the south-east. Fine examples of corrie-lochs are found in the Cairngorms.

The north-eastern and south-western sea-margins of the area are totally different in character (Fig. 1). On the north-east, the straight coast of the Moray Firth probably follows the strikes of the planes of unconformity at the bases of the Triassic and of the Middle and Upper Old Red Sandstone of the district. On the south-west, the most remarkable feature of the coast is the long, narrow fiords that run far into the interior. These have been attributed to erosion along intersecting fractures (Gregory 1913), but the more general view regards them as submerged land valleys overdeepened by ice-erosion during the Glacial period.

## Scenery

Two contrasted types of mountain-scenery are presented by the Grampian Highlands. In the Cairngorm area and around Glen Clova great relics of the peneplain remain as broad, level moorlands cut into by deep glens and scarred by gigantic corrie-cliffs. Towards the south-west this type of mountain-scenery gradually passes into a more highly dissected type of rugged pinnacles, crests and ridges. The detail of this latter form depends upon the geological character and structure of the rocks. Resistant beds, such as quartzites, grits (Plate IIA) or massive gneisses, rise into lofty summits. If no marked guiding planes are present, conical forms result, as in the quartzite mountains of Schichallion, Ben-y-Gloe and Paps of Jura. A series of metamorphosed grits—the Dalradian Upper Psammitic Group—makes a line of conspicuous mountains close to the Highland Boundary Fault; prominent peaks in this line are Ben Vorlich, Ben Ledi and Ben Lomond. Between these resistant quartzites, grits and gneisses, belts of weaker strata such as slates, limestones and phyllites have been excavated into valleys. The tors, scree-slopes and savage corries of the Cairngorms and Lochnagar exemplify the mode of denudation of the granites which form these mountain groups. The bold cliff scenery of Glen Coe, Ben Nevis and adjacent regions is carved out of volcanic rocks or larger granitic masses (Frontispiece and Plate VIII).

### SELECTED REFERENCES*

* A work by one author commonly deals with several subjects described separately in the following chapters of this handbook. In order to avoid needless repetition of the full title only abbreviated references are given at the end of each chapter. The full titles can be found in the General Bibliography at the end of this handbook, against the name of the author and date of the publication.

Alexander, H. 1950; Bailey, E. B. 1934a; Bailey, E. B. 1960; Bremner, A. 1915, 1919, 1942; Cadell, H. M. 1886, 1913; Geikie, A. 1901; George, T. N. 1955, 1960; Gibb, A. W. 1909; Gregory, J. W. 1913; Hinxman, L. W. 1901; Linton, D. L. 1951; Mackinder, H. J. 1907; Munro, H. T. and others 1953; Peach, B. N. and Horne, J. 1910, 1930.

PLATE I. The South-west Grampians

# 2. SUMMARY OF GEOLOGY

## AND TABLE OF FORMATIONS

The oldest rocks of the region described are found on Islay and Colonsay, on the extreme western margin of the area. They belong to the Lewisian Metamorphic Assemblage of the Archaean basement and are directly overlain by sediments which are thought to belong to the Torridonian System. By analogy with their counterparts in the Northern Highlands these ancient rocks together may make up a fragment of the stable shield area which borders the western seaboard of Scotland but their total outcrop is too small for their regional tectonic setting to be clearly demonstrated.

By far the greatest area of rocks described in the handbook are paraschists which, together with a very limited amount of other strata, represent part of a thick accumulation of sedimentary rocks deposited on the Archaean basement in a complex mobile belt which stretched at least from Scandinavia to Ireland and is probably represented in Spitzbergen and Greenland. To this belt the name 'Caledonian Geosyncline' has been applied. In the Grampian area the rocks of the geosyncline are made up of two contrasting facies; (1) the Moinian Metamorphic Assemblage (the lower group) characterized by uniformity of deposits over great vertical thicknesses, probably representing sediments deposited in the shallow water of a slowly-subsiding area during an early phase of the movements in the mobile belt, and (2) the Dalradian Metamorphic Assemblage (the upper group) characterized by considerable vertical variation of diverse rocks, probably representing sediments accumulating in the later, more rapidly subsiding, geosyncline proper. Rocks of the Moinian Assemblage are at present accepted by most Highland geologists as being, at least in part, contemporaneous with those of the Torridonian System. On this correlation Moinian strata would be of late pre-Cambrian age. The Dalradian rocks range in age from late pre-Cambrian (probably) to at least late Lower Cambrian and are essentially conformable on the Moinian Assemblage although the stratigraphical relationships of the two assemblages are not known with absolute certainty (see p. 31).

An orogeny associated with the geosyncline folded the strata deposited in it. The deformation during this folding was polyphase, but the general term 'Caledonian Orogeny' has been applied to it and the name 'Caledonides' was given by E. Suess to the mountain chain which, he inferred, arose as a result. It is doubtful if any single chain of fold-mountains extended over the whole area of the geosyncline at any one time, and it is likely that the metamorphic rocks of the northern and north-western part of the Caledonian fold-belt formed a chain of 'Early Caledonides' (H. H. Read 1961) in which the movements were pre-Silurian (possibly pre-Arenig), in contrast to the remainder of the belt, comprising non-metamorphic (or at the most lightly metamorphosed) rocks, in which the main folding was of late-Silurian age, possibly continuing to mid-Devonian. The metamorphic rocks of the Grampians form part of these Early Caledonides and, for brevity, will be referred to in this handbook

5

TABLE I

## GEOLOGICAL TABLE OF THE ROCKS IN THE GRAMPIAN HIGHLANDS OF SCOTLAND

| Era | Period | Rocks | IGNEOUS ROCKS — CONTEMPORANEOUS | IGNEOUS ROCKS — INTRUSIVE | MIGMATITES |
|---|---|---|---|---|---|
| QUATERNARY | Recent and Pleistocene *(Superficial Deposits)* | Blown Sand; Peat; Fresh Water Alluvium along Rivers; Marine Alluvia, including Raised Beach Deposits; Fluvio-Glacial Sands and Gravels } *Glacial Deposits*; Moraines of Valley Glaciers; Morainic Drift and Boulder Clay | | | |
| TERTIARY | ? Pliocene | Gravels and Clays of the Buchan District | | Basalt and Dolerite Dykes | |
| MESOZOIC AND UPPER PALAEOZOIC | Jurassic | Sandstones, Clays, Mudstones | | | |
| | Permian and Triassic | Sandstones | | Camptonitic Dykes and Vent *(Late Carboniferous or Permian)* | |
| | Carboniferous | *'Millstone Grit' and Coal Measures'* Coal, Sandstones,; *'Carboniferous Limestone Series'* Shales, Limestones, etc.; *'Calciferous Sandstone Series'* Conglomerates, etc. | Basaltic Lavas; Basaltic Lavas | Quartz-dolerite Dykes *('Permo-Carboniferous')* | |
| PALAEOZOIC | Old Red Sandstone — *Upper Old Red Sandstone; Middle Old Red Sandstone; Lower Old Red Sandstone* | Conglomerates, Breccia, Sandstones, Shales, Limestones, etc. | Andesitic Lavas and Andesitic and other Lavas and Pyroclastic Rocks *(of 'Newer Igneous' suite)* | **Caledonian Suite** — NEWER IGNEOUS INTRUSIONS' comprising 1) Post-tectonic cauldron-subsidence granitic plutons and associated hypabyssal rocks, probably of Lower Old Red Sandstone age; 2) Late-to post-tectonic basic, granitic or complex plutons and hypabyssal rocks, mainly pre-Lower Old Red Sandstone age | |
| LOWER PALAEOZOIC | Cambro-Ordovician | Grits, Conglomerates, Limestones, Black Shales, Cherts, Jasper | Spilitic Lavas | | |
| Metamorphic Rocks of the Grampian Caledonides ? 'Late Pre-Cambrian to Cambrian' | Dalradian | Schists representing:- Siliceous Sandstones, Sandstones, Greywackes, Shales, Limestones, etc. | Metamorphosed Lavas (mainly Spilitic) and ? Tuffs *(of 'Older Igneous' suite)* | 'OLDER IGNEOUS INTRUSIONS' comprising pre- or early-tectonic basic and granitic plutons and lesser masses, possibly ranging from late pre-Cambrian to early Ordovician | Syntectonic Migmatites |
| | Moinian | Schists representing:- Siliceous Sandstones, Sandstones, Shales | | | |
| ARCHAEOZOIC | Torridonian — *? Applecross; Diabaig* | Grits, Sandstones, Conglomerates, Shales (more or less altered) | | | |
| ARCHAEAN | Lewisian | Gneisses of uncertain or mixed origin | ? | Basic Dykes; Granite Pegmatite Veins | ? |

The Caledonian Orogeny is taken to have been instituted in *post-Cambrian/pre-Silurian* times. Over most of the Grampian region, the main movements appear to have been *pre-Lower Old Red Sandstone.*

as the 'Grampian Caledonides'. In them the main tectonic episode was over prior to the deposition of the Lower Old Red Sandstone. In the Early Caledonides one phase of the folding was characterized by recumbent-folds and nappes resembling structures found in the Alps and other mountain ranges of the present day, suggesting that in the Scottish Highlands at least a mountain chain of Alpine dimensions once existed.

Associated with the Caledonian Orogeny is a great suite of igneous rocks, both intrusive and extrusive. In the Grampians, the representatives of this suite make up a considerable proportion of the area and comprise members which, with respect to the Early Caledonides, are pre- and early-tectonic, late-tectonic and post-tectonic. Syntectonic migmatites are extensively developed. The pre- and early-tectonic group, now found mainly as hornblende-schists and epidiorites, were probably basic intrusions and lavas, the syntectonic migmatite complexes are granitic or granodioritic while the late and post-tectonic igneous activity is represented by basic or acid plutons and plutonic complexes together with minor intrusions and some lavas, the igneous activity extending at least well into Lower Old Red Sandstone times.

The metamorphic rocks comprising the Grampian Caledonides, together with some Cambro-Ordovician strata found along the Highland Border, are overlain by rocks of the Old Red Sandstone System whose sediments probably represent debris from the erosion of the mountain chain, thus being analagous to the Alpine 'molasse'. Lavas of the post-tectonic igneous activity referred to above are interbedded with Lower Old Red Sandstone sediments and both arc locally involved in cauldron-subsidences associated with granitic plutonic ring-complexes of considerable size. The Highland Boundary Fault became important in Old Red Sandstone times, throwing Lower Old Red Sandstone sediments down against the metamorphic rocks. About this period too, movement was probably instituted along some of the large-scale wrench-faults which traverse the Grampians in a north-north-easterly direction.

From Old Red Sandstone times onwards the Grampian Highlands were not involved in any major folding. Later movements appear to have been confined to broad folding, elevation and depression, or displacement along faults (in the case of wrench-faults very considerable displacement) of a relatively stable block comprising the metamorphic rocks and overlying sediments. These sediments range in age from Old Red Sandstone to Recent, but, apart from the former, only Permo-Triassic rocks are now represented to any notable extent, much of the original sedimentary cover to the schists having been removed during one or other of several periods of erosion which took place during the long post-Old Red Sandstone history of the region. Igneous rocks of the Carboniferous, Permo-Carboniferous and Tertiary suites, however, are represented by minor intrusions.

### REFERENCES

Johnson, M. R. W. and Stewart, F. H. 1963; Read, H. H. 1961; Suess, E. 1904. Geological Survey Memoirs have been published describing the geology of many of the one-inch maps listed below. For a list of these see the General Bibliography at the end of this Guide.

GEOLOGICAL SURVEY MAPS OF THE GRAMPIAN HIGHLANDS
*On the scale of* 1 *inch to* 1 *mile*

*Colour-printed:* Sheets 19 (Bowmore); 27 (Portaskaig); 28 (Jura); 35 (Colonsay); 36 (Kilmartin); 37 (Inverary); 44 (Mull); 45 (Oban); 53 (Ben Nevis); 54 (Rannoch); 55 (Blair Athole); 64 (Kingussie); 65 (Balmoral); 67 (Stonehaven); 74 (Grantown-on-Spey); 83 (Inverness); 84 (Nairn); 86 (Huntly); 96 (Banff).

*Hand-coloured:* Sheets 12 (Campbeltown); 20 (Killearn); 29 (Rothesay); 38 (Loch Lomond); 46 (Balquhidder); 47 (Crieff); 56 (Blairgowrie); 57 (Forfar); 66 (Banchory); 75 (Tomintoul); 76 (Inverurie); 77 (Aberdeen); 85 (Rothes); 87 (Peterhead); 94 (Cromarty); 95 (Elgin); 97 (Fraserburgh).

The colour-printed sheets are either currently in print or will shortly be available and can be had from any Ordnance Survey Agent. The older, hand-coloured, sheets are out of print, but photostatic or photographic copies (black and white) can be had at a small charge on request from:

The Assistant Director,
Geological Survey of Great Britain,
19 Grange Terrace,
Edinburgh, 9,
Scotland.

*On the scale of ¼ inch to 1 mile:*
Sheets 9 (Aberdeenshire and Banffshire); 12 (Forfar and Kincardine); 13 (Islay Archipelago); 14 (Firth of Clyde); 16 (South Kintyre).

*Other maps*
Tectonic Map of Great Britain and Northern Ireland, 1 : 1 584 000.
Geological Survey 'Ten Mile' Map of Great Britain (1 : 625 000), Sheet One.
6 inches to 1 mile maps of many areas are deposited for reference at the above address.

# 3. THE LEWISIAN AND TORRIDONIAN ROCKS
## OF ISLAY AND COLONSAY

## Introduction

Rocks which can be referred with considerable confidence to the Lewisian Assemblage and to the Torridonian System are found in Islay and Colonsay, together with certain strata (the Bowmore Sandstone of Islay) whose affinities are less certain but which are generally taken to be Torridonian. In Islay, these ancient rocks lie to the west of the Loch Skerrols Thrust (Fig. 2), which separates them from the Dalradian strata of the Grampian Caledonides making up the eastern part of the island. If one believes that the Loch Skerrols Thrust is in fact the Moine Thrust (Bailey 1917; Kennedy 1946) then the pattern of outcrops of the area bears a strong resemblance to that of the North-west Highlands (*see*, for instance, Phemister 1960). On this hypothesis the Lewisian and Torridonian rocks occupy the same relative position as do their counterparts in the 'foreland' area of the North-west, the adjacent portion of the Caledonides being made up of Moinian strata in that district but of Dalradian rocks in Islay.

As the Islay and Colonsay rocks lie far from the 'type' outcrops of the North-west Highlands the above hypothesis is, of course, rather tentative and three other possible tectonic settings for the rocks may be considered here:

(1) The Lewisian and Torridonian may not make up a fragment of true foreland, but could be part of a tectonic slice in the region of the Caledonian Mountain Front, similar to the Tarskavaig or Kishorn nappes of the North-west Highlands. The fact that the Islay and Colonsay rocks have been involved in post-Torridonian, probably Caledonian, movements and metamorphism, tends to support this suggestion. Indeed B. N. Peach (1930) pointed out resemblances between the Torridonian of the present area and rocks of the Coulin Forest (Kishorn Nappe) of Ross-shire.

(2) The Loch Skerrols Thrust need not be the Moine Thrust, but could be a structurally higher plane of movement. It could well represent the Iltay Boundary Slide, an important structure which traverses the Grampian Caledonides (p. 15). This is the most recent view of E. B. Bailey (*see* Read and MacGregor 1948, p. 33), and it implies that the Dalradian rocks of Eastern Islay have over-ridden the Moine Thrust. This view has been accepted in this handbook as a basis for the description of the structures of the Grampian Caledonides.

(3) The Torridonian rocks of the Rhinns of Islay, Oronsay (a small island barely separated from Colonsay) and Colonsay apparently form a continuously ascending sequence. The Bowmore Sandstone, on the other hand, is not clearly part of this sequence and lies to the east of a hollow in Islay in which lie Loch Indaal and Loch Gruinart. It is possible that this hollow marks the line of a fault, the Loch Gruinart Fault, thus accounting for the uncertain stratigraphical position of the Bowmore rocks. Some authors,

indeed, have considered that the Loch Gruinart Fault is the Great Glen Fault and, if this were the case the proposed tectonic setting for the Islay and Colonsay rocks would need to be considerably modified. W. Q. Kennedy who has made a study of the Great Glen Fault (1946) considered the correlation of the Loch Gruinart and Great Glen faults to be unlikely and his view that the latter passes north of Colonsay is now generally accepted.

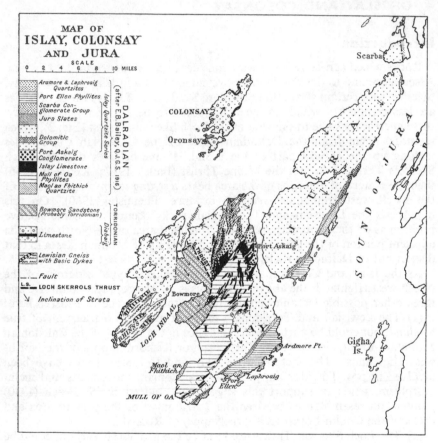

FIG. 2. *Geological map of Islay, Colonsay and Jura*

The doubtful stratigraphical position of the Bowmore Sandstone at one time gave rise to much speculation as to whether it was Torridonian, 'Moinian' or 'Dalradian'. Most of the arguments against its Torridonian age are no longer valid in the light of the probable equivalence of that System and part of the Moinian Assemblage and for the purposes of this account the Torridonian age is accepted (Fig. 2).

## Lewisian

Rocks referred on lithological grounds to the Lewisian occupy an area of less than twenty square miles in the Rhinns of Islay, where they are overlain by strata considered to be Torridonian. At the north end of Colonsay is seen a tiny area of Lewisian rocks, less than one-eighth of a square mile in size. In both islands, the marginal relations of the two formations are complicated by shearing or folding.

The Lewisian rocks of Islay consist of acid and basic igneous gneisses. The original rocks were probably biotite- and hornblende-gneisses like those found in the Lewisian Gneiss of the North-west Highlands, but they are now microbreccias and show a cataclastic metamorphism characterized by granulation and mylonization, similar to that produced by the post-Cambrian (Caledonian) movements in the North-west Highlands. These gneisses are cut by a series of basic intrusions, comprising epidiorite, hornblende-schist, diorite, augite-diorite, and augite-hypersthene-diorite.

The Lewisian Gneisses of Colonsay are coarse-grained banded quartzo-feldspathic rocks with dark knots and streaks. The principal rock-types are amphibolites, hornblende-gneisses, biotite-gneisses and pegmatite. Like the Islay rocks, they show cataclastic shattering.

## Torridonian

The general consensus of opinion has long regarded the correlation of the sedimentary rocks of the northern part of the Rhinns of Islay, Oronsay and Colonsay with the Torridonian as extremely probable and this view has recently been endorsed by A. D. Stewart (1962a; b). As stated earlier there is at present no reason to doubt that the Bowmore Sandstone is other than Torridonian.

In the Geological Survey Memoir the sedimentary rocks of the Rhinns of Islay and Bowmore were grouped by S. B. Wilkinson as follows:

Applecross Division
{ *Bowmore Grits (or Sandstone):* red, green and grey grits or arkose, in places very coarse grained and containing pebbles of quartzite, felsite, granite, etc.—*Blackrock Pebble Bed.*

Diabaig Division
{ *Kilchiaran Slate and Grit Series:* grey green and black slates and phyllites alternating with grey schistose grit and thin bands of sandy limestone.
*Rhinns Conglomerate Series:* schistose epidotic grits, thin phyllite bands, and local conglomerate.

The allocation of the Bowmore rocks to the Applecross Group is rather tentative and Stewart (1962b) noted a similarity between them and certain dark coloured Diabaig rocks in Skye and Iona.

In Colonsay and Oronsay the succession (Geological Survey Memoir; Stewart 1962a) is as follows:

8. Staosnaig Phyllite Group: dark phyllites.
7. Colonsay Limestone Group: dark sandy limestone on east coast; two limestones separated by dark phyllites and flags at Kiloran Bay.
6. Kiloran Flag Group: very uniform and constant.
5. Milbuie Group: epidotic grits, grits and phyllites.
4. Kilchattan Group: phyllite and sandstone, greatly varying.
3. Machrins Group: alternating grits and mudstones.
2. Dun Gallain Group: epidotic grits, in places interdigitating with Group 3.
1. Oronsay (Greywacke) Group: sandstones below, mudstones above.

Stewart followed the Geological Survey in considering that the Oronsay Group is an extension of the Kilchiaran Slate and Grit Series, and allocated all the Colonsay, Oronsay and Rhinns of Islay Torridonian rocks to the Diabaig Division, comparing them with Diabaig rocks of Skye, Loch Carron and Iona. As mentioned above he also compared the Bowmore Sandstone with certain Diabaig strata.

Stewart estimated the total thickness of the Torridonian rocks to be in excess of 4 km. of which 2+ km. are made up of the Kilchiaran and Oronsay groups. Rocks of these latter groups he considered to be greywackes of turbidite type, overlain with slight unconformity by the Dun Gallain Group.

Like the Lewisian of the area the Torridonian rocks have been folded and metamorphosed by movements which are probably of Caledonian age. The degree of metamorphism of the Torridonian rocks is not high, the strata being folded and cleaved but only slightly recrystallized. W. B. Wright (1908) recognized two periods of movement separated by a period of igneous activity during which small syenitic and dioritic masses and many lamprophyre dykes were intruded. Stewart, however, recognized three periods of deformation. During the first period the rocks were cleaved and to some extent recrystallized but no significant folds were formed. During the second large folds were formed and the rocks were again cleaved. The third deformation produced several sets of folds and strain-slip cleavages which are strongly developed only locally.

It should perhaps be mentioned here that B. N. Peach (1930) correlated the Colonsay Torridonian with the Islay Dalradian. Quite apart from the fact that this is not in accord with modern ideas concerning Torridonian-Moinian-Dalradian relationships, E. B. Bailey and W. B. Wright, in the Geological Survey Memoir on Colonsay, had already shown that on the basis of stratigraphical comparisons, the correlation was extremely unlikely.

## REFERENCES

Bailey, E. B. 1917; Elles, Gertrude L. and Tilley, C. E. 1930; Green, J. F. N. 1924; Gregory, J. W. 1930; Kennedy, W. Q. 1946; Peach, B. N. and Horne, J. 1930; Phemister, J. 1960; Read, H. H. and MacGregor, A. G. 1948; Stewart, A. D. 1962a, 1962b; Wright, W. B. 1908.

*Geological Survey Memoirs* 'The Geology of Islay, etc.'; 'The Geology of Colonsay and Oronsay, etc.'

PLATE II

A. Mountains formed from schistose grit

B. Ben Lawers and Loch Tay

PLATE III

A. Current-bedding in quartzite

B. Folding and cleavage in schistose rocks

PLATE IV

A. Large scale folding in Dalradian rocks

B. Loch Leven and the Mamore Hills

# 4. THE GRAMPIAN CALEDONIDES
## PART I: INTRODUCTION

The structure and stratigraphy of the Grampian Caledonides long defied analysis and much controversy as to the original order of deposition of the strata characterized discussions on the geology of the region from the 1890's to 1930. The main cause of this controversy was the lack of reliable data which might indicate whether the succession is (a) right way up, (b) inverted, as in the limb of a large overturned fold (such folds being locally demonstrable on the ground), or (c) a reduplication of strata by numerous isoclinal folds. Lack of this essential key led to widely different interpretations of local successions, of tectonics, and even of the distribution of metamorphic zones. The 'way-up' criterion of current-bedding orientation was applied in Scotland as early as 1924, but was not widely known until it was demonstrated in Lochaber in 1929 and used to show folding in the *inverted* limb of an extensive recumbent fold (Vogt 1930; Bailey 1930). This spectacular application of the technique initiated a new era in Highland research. Other criteria of the relative ages of successive beds, such as graded-bedding and various sedimentation structures have since been employed and local sequences can now be correlated with considerable confidence throughout wide areas of the Grampians (Plate IIIA). Way-up criteria in many instances can be used also as a cross-check on proposed structural inversions and the anticlinal or synclinal nature of large recumbent folds can be made out.

A large measure of structural and stratigraphical agreement has now been reached which replaces the disagreements of former years and, although controversy is by no means over, it is now possible to give a synthesis which is basically accepted by most working Highland geologists.

The portion of the Scottish Caledonides which is represented in the Grampian Highlands comprises both metamorphic rocks and others which, except for a dynamically-imposed cleavage, are virtually non-metamorphic, the former having by far the greater outcrop. Most of the area is made up from members of the Moinian and Dalradian Metamorphic assemblages (Anderson 1948), but as there has been considerable dubiety as to what constitutes the Dalradian, a brief account of origin of the name is given below.

In 1891 Sir A. Geikie pointed out that the varied group of metamorphic rocks which lies to the east of the Great Glen was likely to be younger than the Lewisian Gneiss of the North-west Highlands. For these younger rocks he coined the name 'Dalradian' (derived from the ancient Scottish kingdom of Dalriada), although he carefully pointed out that in proposing this name he was not founding a new geological system, but merely providing a convenient term to be used while the true affinities of the rocks were being sought. The 1892 and 1910 editions of Bartholomew's 10-miles-to-an-inch Geological Map of Scotland (compiled under Geikie's direction) however, extended the name 'Dalradian' to include *all the metamorphic strata east of the Moine Thrust*, although in his Explanatory Notes to the map (1892) Geikie clearly considered the 'Moine Schists' of the Northern Highlands to be different in character from the 'Dalradian' rocks south-east of the Great Glen. As research proceeded, it became apparent that, as Geikie suspected, rocks of this 'Moine Schist' facies could be identified in the latter area, leaving as 'Dalradian' a rather characteristic assemblage of rocks lying mainly in the south-west and south-east part of the Grampians. In addition it was found that the 'Moine Schists' (now Moinian Assemblage) were not of mixed origin as Geikie and his colleagues thought, but, like the Dalradian, were metamorphosed sedimentary rocks. The two assemblages were found to be notably contrasted, the Moinian consisting mainly of psammitic and pelitic rocks which, over much of Scotland, and especially in the Grampians, are thickly stratified (see Ch. 6) while the Dalradian rocks were not only lithologically diverse but in places form relatively thin groups and clearly originated in a depositional environment different from that of the Moines.

Differing usage of the name 'Dalradian' through the years, combined with lack of sufficient stratigraphical information concerning Moine–Dalradian relationships, has led to some difference of opinion as to where, in the stratigraphical column, the Dalradian rocks commence (e.g. Anderson 1948, 1953). In this account, following Geological Survey practice and much published work, the base of the Dalradian Assemblage is taken at the lowest of the series of diversified rocks which apparently stratigraphically overlie the Central Highland Granulites (see p. 34). Anderson (1948) pointed out certain anomalies which arise from this classification, but it still seems to be the most useful one.

Over much of its outcrop the Moine–Dalradian junction is either tectonic (see below) or intricately interfolded, and until these factors were recognized much controversy took place as to the relationships between the two assemblages. Indeed, the position is not yet altogether clear. On a broad scale the Dalradian overlies the Moinian and, in certain sections where the rocks are probably not in tectonic contact, the older members of the Dalradian sequence (as the term is used here) can clearly be shown by sedimentary way-up criteria to be younger than the contiguous Moinian rocks (e.g. Anderson 1948; Bailey 1934; Anderson 1956). In some of these exposures there is reasonable evidence for sedimentary passage between rocks of the two assemblages (Bailey 1934, p. 499; Anderson 1956) and this suggests at least that no great unconformity exists between them. The Dalradian Assemblage is thus generally taken to be a group of rocks younger than the Moines. Exposures of unmoved contacts are so few, however, that no firm conclusions can be arrived at as to whether the Dalradian rocks (a) lie completely conformably on the Moinian Assemblage, (b) lie disconformably on it, or (c) are to some extent diachronous with the upper Moinian rocks.

In the Northern Highlands of Scotland inliers of Lewisian strata appear within the area of the Caledonides but no similar major outcrops of rocks of the Lewisian Assemblage are known from the Grampians. In one small area near Fort Augustus, however, certain rocks have been likened to Lewisian types.

The structural interpretation of the Grampian Caledonides is based on the proposals advanced by E. B. Bailey, in part incorporating the work of C. T. Clough and others. In a series of papers from 1910 onwards he showed that the rocks of the South-west Highlands of Scotland are disposed in vast recumbent folds, the limbs of which may be partly replaced by 'slides'—special types of low-angle faults, associated with recumbent folds, whereon overlying strata may have been transported over the underlying rocks for considerable distances. By the introduction of the concept of slides, structural and stratigraphical anomalies could be accounted for on the postulate that rocks and structures, once widely separate, have been 'slid' into juxtaposition. The recognition of these structures, made at a time when the use of 'way-up' criteria was unknown, must be regarded as one of the outstanding achievements of Scottish geology. Bailey (1922) further suggested that in the South-west Highlands these folded rocks could be referred to one or other of three major superimposed structural units, the upper two of which were immense transported sheets, similar to the Alpine 'nappes de charriage', overlying major slides of fundamental importance. It soon became apparent that, in general, this synthesis could be applied to the whole of the Grampian Caledonides.

This threefold major division was modified when Bailey (*in* Allison 1940) accepted the view, developed since his 1922 proposals by several other investigators (e.g. Peach 1930; Elles and Tilley 1930; Allison 1940), that only two major units were involved and until recently, these units have formed the basis of Grampian Highland structural synthesis. The units were the *Iltay Nappe*, a great transported structural complex which made up most of the Southern Grampians from *Isl*ay to Loch *Tay* and thence probably to Deeside. This nappe was thought to overlie both the *Iltay Slide* of the South-west Highlands and its north-eastern continuation, the *Boundary Slide* of the Schichallion district, and the two together have become known as the *Iltay Boundary Slide*. The Iltay Boundary Slide separated the Iltay Nappe from the other major unit—the *Ballappel Foundation* (*Ball*achulish–*App*in–Loch *Eil*de, in the district of Lochaber). This latter unit Bailey only defined in the South-west Highlands area, but the name has since been used to comprise all rocks of the Northern Grampians below the level of the Iltay Boundary Slide.

The Iltay Nappe comprised only Dalradian strata (as the term is used here). The Ballappel Foundation comprised interfolded Dalradian and Moinian rocks.

Bailey's (1922) original conception of the Iltay Nappe was a relatively simple structure comprising rocks which were in part involved in a vast recumbent anticline (the Carrick Castle Fold of C. T. Clough 1897) and in part lay beyond its limits. All these rocks were considered to lie above a common plane of transport—the Iltay Boundary Slide, which he thought of as underlying most of the Southern Grampians. It has become apparent (in part resulting from later work by Bailey himself) that the rocks of the Southern Grampians in fact make up a nappe-complex (MacGregor *in* Read and MacGregor 1948, p. 31; Shackleton 1958, p. 383) and that the term 'Iltay Nappe' can only be maintained if the Slide does in fact underlie the whole of the area defining a vast 'nappe de charriage'. As this cannot be proved it would seem that the term Iltay Nappe were best abandoned. MacGregor used the name 'Iltay Nappe-Complex' but as the structures go well beyond the range implied by the geographical mnemonic the term *Southern Grampians Nappe-Complex* is here preferred. For brevity 'Southern Complex' is used when the context is known. By analogy the term *Northern Grampians Nappe-Complex* (Northern Complex) is employed for the Ballappel Foundation of

Lochaber and its presumed structural continuation further to the north-east,
the original geographical mnemonic being hardly adequate to describe the
whole area.  It will be pointed out (p. 23) that to describe the recumbent folds
of this district as nappes or nappe-folds may not be strictly accurate, but the
terms are convenient and are used in a general manner.

The structural identity of the two complexes is only clear in so far as they are
separated by the Iltay Boundary Slide.  The outcrop of this structure can be
traced (or inferred) possibly from Islay, where it may well be the Loch

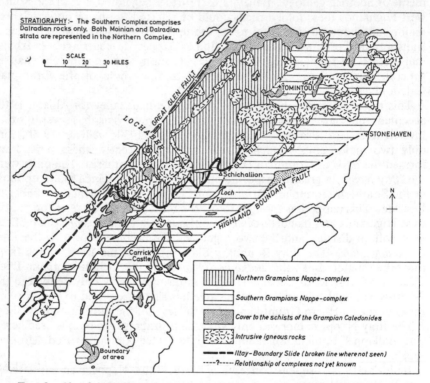

FIG. 3. *Sketch map showing the two main structural divisions of the Grampian
Caledonides*

Skerrols Thrust (p. 9), by way of South Appin to near Glen Tilt.  North-
eastwards therefrom its presence has not as yet been proved (see however
p. 20) and the relationship between the two complexes is therefore uncertain
between Glen Tilt and the north-eastern coast of Scotland (Fig. 3).  In the
Tomintoul area McIntyre (1951) identified slides at or near the base of the
Dalradian sequence.

The folds and slides which go to form these nappe-complexes were
developed during the earliest known fold phases of the Caledonian Orogeny
in each area (see, however, p. 26).  These early folds have a 'Caledonoid'
trend, i.e. from north-east to south-west, parallel to the long axis of the
geosyncline.  They are here referred to as *Early Caledonoid Folds*.  Each
nappe-complex has been considerably re-folded during at least two later fold
phases—the *Transverse Folds*, during which major structures were formed at

high angles to the Caledonoid trend, and the *Late Caledonoid Folds* when the folding once more trended parallel to the long axis of the geosyncline. In each of these fold phases the major folds were accompanied by lesser folds on all scales and, where the movements were intense, resulted in the production of new schistosities in the rocks involved (Plate IIIB).

The anatomy of the Grampian Highlands is best considered with reference to the folds produced during the successive phases, and this plan is followed in the next chapter.

### REFERENCES

Allison, A. 1940; Anderson, J. G. C. 1948, 1953, 1956; Bailey, E. B. 1922, 1930, 1934b; Bailey, E. B. and Holtedahl, O. 1938; Clough, C. T. (*in* Gunn, W. and others) 1897; Elles, Gertrude L. and Tilley, C. E. 1930; Geikie, A. 1891, 1892; MacGregor, A. G. (*in* Read and MacGregor) 1948; McIntyre, D. B. 1951; MacNair, P. 1908; Peach, B. N. and Horne, J. 1930; Shackleton, R. M. 1958; Vogt, T. 1930; Watson, Janet 1963.

## THE GRAMPIAN HIGHLANDS,  Chapters 5 and 6
## IMPORTANT NOTE

The structure and stratigraphy described in this volume is based on the hypothesis current at the time of writing that the Iltay Slide in the south-west part of the area separated the Southern Grampians Nappe Complex from the "Ballappel" area. As a result the correlation of the rocks of the latter area with those of the Southern Grampians was in doubt, but was possibly as shown on Table II (p. 32). Recent work by Rast and Litherland in Islay and Appin strongly suggests that the Ballappel succession is a downward continuation of that of Loch Awe and Islay and that the rocks including and below the Cuil Bay Slates in the Ballachulish and Lochaber sequence are represented in the Mull of Oa Phyllites and Moal an Fhithich Quartzite of Islay.

The Blair Atholl Series of Central Perthshire is the equivalent of the Islay Limestone plus the Cuil Bay Slates in the following manner:

| *Islay* | *Blair Atholl* |
|---|---|
| Islay Limestone | White Limestone |
| Mullach Dubh Phyllites | Banded Group |
| Lismore Limestone | Dark Limestone |
| Cuil Bay Slates | Dark Schist |

These correlations call in question the detailed structure and hence the fundamental significance of the Ballachulish Nappe as described by Bailey.

The above proposals provide an elegant answer to several problems concerning the geology of the area, notably discrepancies between the original Geological Survey maps and the interpretation of the stratigraphy of Appin suggested by Bailey, and the difficulties experienced by Voll (1960) in accepting the detailed structure of Appin. Voll's explanations, however, are now superseded.

Chapters 5 and 6 of this Handbook should, therefore, be read with the new interpretation in mind and the reader is referred to the paper by Rast and Litherland (Geol. Mag., **107, p. 259**) for further details.

# 5. THE GRAMPIAN CALEDONIDES

## PART II: STRUCTURE[1]

## Early Caledonoid Folds—The Nappe-Complexes

### The Southern Grampians Nappe-Complex (The 'Iltay Nappe')

The Southern Grampians Nappe-Complex comprises all the metamorphic rocks between the Iltay Boundary Slide and the Highland Border and, in the North-east Grampians where the slide is unknown, includes all rocks involved in the major early structures continued from the clearly limited area to the south-west. As so defined only Dalradian strata (as the term is used in this handbook) crop out within the area of the Complex, with the possible exception of some Moinian fold cores in the region where the Iltay Boundary Slide is not proved.

The complex is here regarded as consisting of two main sub-units. (a) A transported sheet (comprising several folds) which is contiguous to the out-crop of, and overlies, the Iltay Boundary Slide. Within this sheet all early-formed recumbent anticlines so far recorded close to the north-west. The sheet is here referred to as the *Northern Nappe-zone*. (b) An immense early-formed recumbent anticline, closing to the south-east, which makes up the remainder of the Southern Grampians. This is the *Tay Nappe* (Shackleton 1958). The distribution of these structures is shown on Plate V.

### The Tay Nappe

Satisfactory direct evidence for the presence of a large north-westward-closing recumbent *syncline* in the Southern Grampians Nappe-Complex can be seen at Ben Lui (Bailey 1922; Cummins and Shackleton 1955). This is the *Ben Lui Recumbent Syncline* or the *Ben Lui Fold*.* The strata in the upper limb of this fold, of course, are in inverted stratigraphical succession and south-east from the fold axis the rocks are therefore said to lie in the *Loch Tay Inversion*, which makes up much of the Southern Grampians. In the Pitlochry–Kirkmichael area Bailey (1925) postulated that these inverted rocks form the upper limb of the Pitlochry–Kirkmichael Fold (a recumbent syncline) which thus corresponds to the Ben Lui Fold, and in the following account the whole structure is called the *Ben Lui–Kirkmichael Fold*. It would be expected that overlying the Ben Lui–Kirkmichael Fold a corresponding south-eastward-closing recumbent anticline would right the stratigraphical sequence and it was long thought that this role was fulfilled by the Carrick Castle Fold of C. T. Clough (see Ch. 4). Shackleton (1958) has suggested that the righting anticline is in fact a much larger structure, extending to a closure in the Highland Border area and has given the name *Tay Nappe* to this recumbent fold. This view is taken here as a basis for description. Much of the Tay

---

Nappe has been removed by erosion, but its former presence over most of the Southern Highlands can be inferred from its remnants. For instance, its roots can be seen north-east of the axis of the Ben Lui–Kirkmichael Fold in the *Rha Chreag Anticline* (Elles and Tilley 1930) overlying the Ben Lui Fold, and in the *Creag na h'Iolaire Anticline* (Sturt 1961) overlying the Pitlochry–Kirkmichael Fold. Along the Highland Border a fold, whose presence is confirmed by graded-bedding evidence, is currently taken, following Shackleton, to be the downbent anticlinal closure of the Tay Nappe (Plate V) and is known as the *Aberfoyle Anticline* (see p. 25). In Banff it is likely that a considerable area of rocks, essentially in correct stratigraphical order as shown by way-up structures, makes up a remnant of the upper limb of the Tay Nappe, although possibly displaced on a slide—the *Boyne Lag*. These displaced rocks form the *Banff Nappe* of H. H. Read (1955) although some confusion has arisen as to the correct application of this name. Read himself, in a subsequent paper (1956) applied the term to a huge recumbent structure which is evidently the Tay Nappe. In this account the 1955 usage is followed.

Only one other term in current use need be mentioned in this general account. As the Tay Nappe is a huge, generally flat-lying, recumbent fold, the rocks in it have an overall horizontal disposition, although considerably affected in detail by later folds (p. 24). A large area of the Southern Highlands, made up mainly of the rocks of the Loch Tay Inversion, lie within this '*Flat Belt*'.

As stated earlier, the Tay Nappe Fold is a vast structure. Parallel to its axis, it evidently extends right across Scotland and into Ireland. At high stratigraphical levels it has an amplitude of at least 20 km and probably much more. The fold is disharmonic and thus, at low stratigraphical levels (e.g. in the Rha Chreag area), its amplitude is very much less—of the order of 1 km where last clearly seen in its root zone.

## The Northern Nappe-zone

To what extent the whole Southern Grampians Nappe Complex represents a vast 'nappe de charriage' or transported sheet, everywhere underlain by the Iltay Boundary Slide, is not certain. In the Glen Lyon and Schichallion areas, however, the slide can be shown to underlie the rocks south-east from its outcrop *at least* as far back as the close of the Ben Lui–Kirkmichael Fold (Plate V). North-west from the closure of the latter fold evidence is accumulating that all early-formed *recumbent* anticlines close to the north-west, apparently being genetically related to the underlying slide. South-east from the Ben Lui–Kirkmichael Fold the Tay Nappe (recumbent anticline) closes to the south-east and clearly belongs to a different structural sub-unit (Shackleton 1958, p. 383), whose relation to the Iltay Boundary Slide is problematical. It is therefore a useful concept, if only for the purpose of description, to regard the sheet of rocks transported above the Iltay Boundary Slide and lying north-west of the Ben Lui–Kirkmichael Fold as forming a separate sub-unit of the Southern Grampians Complex, to which the name Northern Nappe-zone is here given.

In the Loch Tummel–Blair Atholl area the rocks of the Northern Nappe-zone are disposed in several nappe-folds which, though large structures measurable in terms of several kilometres, are only of intermediate-scale when compared with the major nappe-folds of both the Northern and Southern complexes. Several of these folds have been named, but they do not merit special description here (Rast 1958; Sturt 1961; Harris A. L. 1963; *also* Bailey 1925, 1928, 1937). As stated above the recumbent anticlines of this group close to the north-west and the folds can be shown (e.g. Rast 1958) to form a 'stacked' pile overlying the Iltay Boundary Slide.

The Northern Nappe-zone is missing from the Loch Lyon district, where erosion has removed the rocks as far back as the Ben Lui–Kirkmichael Fold (Johnstone and Smith 1965) but in Islay and South Lorne there is once more a considerable area of country lying between this Fold and the outcrop of the Iltay Boundary Slide. In this ground the large recumbent Islay Anticline (immediately overlying the Loch Skerrols Thrust) closes to the north-west and, according to Bailey's section (1917, plate xii) appears to be an early structure of nappe-fold (Early Caledonoid fold) age. Over most of South Lorne the strata appear to be essentially right-way-up and no nappe-folds of any size have so far been identified there; early-formed minor recumbent isoclines have, however, been recorded in hydro-electric tunnel sections but the sense of closure of these folds has not been determined. North-eastwards from the Loch Tummel–Blair Atholl area, between Glen Tilt and the north-east coast of Scotland, the structures have not yet been described in detail. Near Braemar Professor B. C. King (personal communication) has identified primary recumbent folds 'in the hinge region of the primary syncline under-lying the anticlinal Tay Nappe'. These structures face south-eastwards, so it would appear that in this area, as in the Loch Lyon district, the northward-closing nappe-zone is missing, perhaps removed by erosion. The Iltay Boundary Slide has not specifically been identified by Professor King, although he has recorded a complex series of slides and thrusts which post-date the main fold movements. In the Banffshire area Dr. F. May, in course of current work for the Geological Survey, has found what appears to be a stacked arrangement of west-closing early-formed recumbent anticlines in close proximity to the Moinian outcrop.

## The zone of divergence

In the two zones of the Southern Grampians Nappe-Complex discussed above, large anticlinal nappe folds close in opposite senses. It is obvious that they must diverge from a medial line and that this line must lie somewhere to the north-west of the Ben Lui–Kirkmichael Fold. In the Tummel area B. A. Sturt (1961) found that this divergence takes place on either side of a mappable synclinal structure, the Sron Mhor Syncline, and suggests that the divergence is marked elsewhere by the similar synclines of Loch Awe and Turriff (or Boyndie). (*See also* Rast, *in* Johnson and Stewart 1963).

## The Northern Grampians Nappe-Complex

The Northern Grampians Nappe-Complex comprises all the metamorphic rocks which lie between the Iltay Boundary Slide and the Great Glen. As in the case of the Southern Complex, its limits cannot clearly be delineated in the north-eastern Grampians where the slide, or its equivalent, has so far not been proved (see Fig. 4).

The structures of the Northern Complex have not yet been sufficiently elucidated for a detailed synthesis to be given, as much of the area is made up of rocks of the Moinian Assemblage where lack of distinctive marker horizons renders investigations difficult. In the south-western part of the region, however, where both Dalradian and Moinian strata are present and interfolded, the structures are known in great detail. This is the area of the 'Ballappel Foundation' of E. B. Bailey. The true relationships of the Ballappel

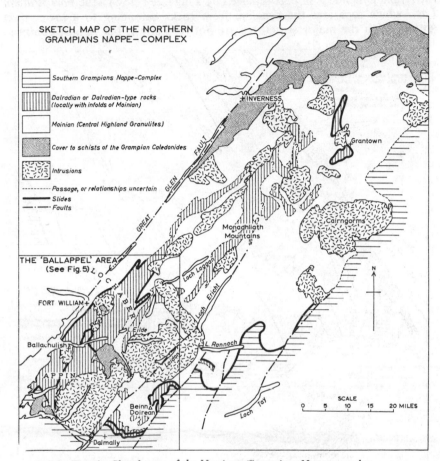

FIG. 4. *Sketch map of the Northern Grampians Nappe-complex*

structures to those which may exist in the north-eastern area has not so far been made out. Indeed, it is by no means certain that the two areas belong to the same structural sub-unit. In this handbook therefore, the Northern Complex will be treated under two geographical headings—The 'Ballappel Area' as described by Bailey in his 1922 synthesis, and the 'Remainder of the Northern Complex'.

## The 'Ballappel' Area (Fig. 5; Plate IVв)

The 'Ballappel' area comprises the metamorphic rocks of Lochaber (east of the Great Glen), Appin, and the Dalmally–Beinn Doirean area.

(1) In the *Lochaber and Appin* district the rocks of the Northern Complex are disposed in a major recumbent anticlinal nappe-fold, apparently closing

to the north-west, and form the *Kinlochleven* (*Recumbent*) *Anticline*. The corresponding underlying syncline is the *Appin* (*Recumbent*) *Syncline*, the limb common to both structures being the *Kinlochleven Inversion* (the terminology being analogous to that for the Tay Nappe). The lower limb of the Appin Syncline is in part replaced by a lag (see below)—the *Fort William Lag*—which separates the syncline from rocks belonging to a lower level within which the major structures are not yet known, but in part comprise

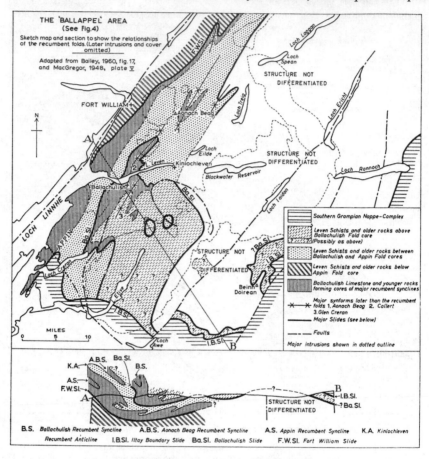

FIG. 5. *Sketch map of structures in the 'Ballappel' area*

Bailey's '*Sub-Eilde Complex*'. In North-east Lochaber the lag may not be present and the continuation of the Ballappel structures into the North-east Grampians is problematical (p. 23). The upper limb of the Kinlochleven Anticline is also in part replaced by a lag—the *Ballachulish Lag*—and this in turn in part replaces the lower limb of the corresponding major synclinal structure above the anticline. This is the *Ballachulish* (*Recumbent*) *Syncline* and is apparently the highest structure exposed in the Ballappel area. It seems likely that at least one anticlinal fold must have righted the stratigraphical succession above the Ballachulish Syncline, but there is as yet no evidence that the right-way-up limb has anywhere been preserved.

In his earlier papers Bailey was uncertain which of his folds in the 'Ballappel' area were anticlines and which were synclines and he used the non-committal term fold-fault, or slide. But in 1922 the available evidence led him to suggest that the Appin and Ballachulish folds were anticlinal 'nappes' with associated thrust-slides; the Kinlochleven fold was, correspondingly, taken to be a syncline. In 1930, however, he applied sedimentary way-up criteria to the rocks and confirmed an alternative stratigraphical hypothesis by R. G. Carruthers. From this the true nature of the folds, as given above, became apparent, with the surprising corollary that the main slides were found to be lag-slides, on which the upper layers of rock instead of being thrust over these underneath, have 'lagged behind' relatively to them; in other words the slides replace the non-inverted limbs of the recumbent synclines. Under these circumstances the Ballachulish and Appin structures cannot strictly be referred to as 'nappes', but as there are obvious analogies between anticlinal nappe-folds and synclinal recumbent folds, it seems reasonable to retain the term Nappe-Complex for the major subdivision of this part of the Grampians.

These huge recumbent structures of Lochaber and Appin are by no means simple folds. Each, in fact, is a fold-complex comprising smaller recumbent folds and attendant slides. Of these smaller folds only one merits special mention as significantly affecting the distribution of the Ballappel strata. This is the *Aonach Beag (Recumbent) Syncline*, which overlies the Kinlochleven Anticline to the north and west of the known limits of the Ballachulish Fold and Lag (Fig. 5).

(2) In the *Dalmally–Beinn Doirean* area, as in Lochaber and Appin, large scale recumbent folds and slides have been recorded—for instance on Beinn Udlaidh and Beinn Doirean (Bailey and Macgregor 1912). Both Moinian and Dalradian rocks are again involved. Bailey tentatively suggested that some of the Dalradian strata of the district lie in the Ballachulish Fold, resting on the Ballachulish Slide (1912; *see also* 1922, plate i), thus necessitating a huge extension of these structures from their Lochaber outcrops. It is not unlikely that the Beinn Doirean rocks form part of the Southern Complex (Johnstone and Smith 1965) and they are therefore shown on Fig. 5, with a separate ornament, as ?Ballachulish Recumbent Syncline, pending further investigation.

### The Remainder of the Northern Complex

Much of the remainder of the Northern Complex is made up of rocks of the Moinian Assemblage the tectonics of which are as yet little known.

In many areas the prevailing flaggy nature of the Grampian Moines can be seen (as in Moinian strata elsewhere in Scotland) to be due to intense repetitive folding and small-scale planar displacement, but it is not yet clear whether these are features associated with large nappe-structures similar to those in the 'Ballappel' area, or whether they represent a type of deformation peculiar to the Moinian rocks (*see* King and Rast 1956).

Over much of the Monadhliath mountains and the Loch Laggan district to the south (Fig. 4), an area contiguous to the recumbently-folded 'Ballappel' district, Anderson (1956) accounted for the distribution of the Monadhliath Schists (p. 31) without invoking more than isoclinal folding. In the Grantown area near Tomintoul, north-east from the Monadhliath, MacIntyre (1951) postulated the presence of large tectonic slices within the Northern Complex.

## Transverse Folds

Following the formation of each complex during the Early Caledonoid fold phase, the rocks were folded about axes whose generalized trend is at high angles to the Caledonoid direction. These are here referred to as Transverse folds. Some authors claim that folds on these axes are coeval with the Early Caledonoid. Locally this may well be the case but in some areas the transverse folds apparently involve strata already folded on the earlier Caledonoid axis. The two lines of evidence need not be incompatible: it is not unlikely that fold regimes may overlap to some extent.

In the Southern Complex the Transverse folds may be of considerable size. In the Schichallion–Glen Errochty area, for instance, a remarkable sideways-closing tightly-compressed fold twists a stacked group of Early Caledonoid folds of the Northern Nappe Zone, together with the (Iltay) Boundary Slide which they overlie. The amplitude of this fold is considerable—about 9 km—and it is the largest of the known transverse structures in the Grampians. Other transverse structures in the Southern Grampians are indicated on Plate V and it is possible that broad culminations of Early Caledonoid folds noted at one or two places, but not shown on the map may also be due to the presence of transverse folds.

In the Northern Complex area individual Transverse folds are not large enough to be shown on Fig. 4. In Lochaber the presence of folds at high angles to the Caledonoid direction has been proved by Weiss and McIntyre (1957) who claimed that they are the earliest detectable structures of the district, but Bailey (1960) suggested that, as in the Southern Complex, the Transverse folds affect strata already folded by the Early Caledonoid nappe-folds described in the foregoing section of this account.

## Late Caledonoid Folds

In both Northern and Southern Complexes the Early Caledonoid and Transverse folds are both involved in a still later fold phase. Folds of this period are, in both cases, once more in a generally north-easterly (Caledonoid) direction. The folding may be intense, but no large recumbent isoclines of this phase have so far been identified, the axial planes of the folds being vertical or steeply-inclined. In the Southern Complex major late folds of Caledonoid trend are generally open structures which may be of considerable size, with axes traceable for tens of kilometres and with a crest-to-crest distance also of the order of several kilometres. A number of them merit special mention (see Plate V).

### The Cowal Anticline (Antiform)

The Cowal Anticline is a well-marked broad arch of foliation trending north-east across the Cowal district of the South-west Highlands. It is of considerable width, extending from Loch Awe on the north-west to the Highland Border on the south-east.

### The Ben Ledi Antiform

North-eastwards from Cowal the broad arch of the Cowal Anticline apparently gives place to a more complex structure. The crest of the arch,

between Glen Dochard–Loch Tay and the Highland Border becomes flat—
the 'Flat Belt' referred to earlier, the equivalent anticlinal effect being given
by a sharp monoclinal downbend only a few kilometres from the Highland
Border—the Ben Ledi Antiform of R. M. Shackleton—together with a well-
marked synform (the Ben Lawers Synform) on the north-west side of the
Flat Belt.

*The Ben Lawers Syncline (Synform)*

The Ben Lawers Syncline of foliation extends north from the Loch Tay
Fault to near Crianlarich. Other, less well-marked, elongated folds of the
same age lie between it and the Iltay Boundary Slide. According to Elles
(1926) several intermediate-scale Early Caledonoid recumbent folds are
folded by this syncline in the type area of Ben Lawers.

*The Loch Awe Syncline (Synform)*

There is some doubt as to the true status of the well-known apparent
syncline of foliation known as the Loch Awe Syncline. It may either represent
the synclinal structure complementary to the Cowal Anticline or may (Sturt
1961) represent a primary syncline in the zone of divergence (p. 20); or it
could be a combination of both.

All the foregoing structures are shown on Plate V. It is possible that in the
North-east Grampians the large depression of the metamorphic strata (the
Turriff Syncline) formed by the Boyndie Syncline, and the Buchan Anticline
may be a Late Caledonoid structure.

In the Northern Complex major Late Caledonoid folds are in general much
more compressed than those of the Southern Complex. Instead of being open
structures they may even be isoclinal and, according to Bailey's sections across
the Ballappel district, some may be considerably overturned (Plate IVB).
Several have been named, The Aonach Beag, Stob Ban, Callert, and Glen
Creran synforms respectively, and are shown on Fig. 4. Folds which may be
of this date form the most notable structures in the Monadhliath area (*see*
Anderson 1956, fig. 1 and plate iv).

# The Aberfoyle Anticline

As the Aberfoyle Anticline is not only of great structural importance, but is
the key to much of the stratigraphy of the Southern Complex it merits more
detailed description than has been given so far. This will also serve to
illustrate some of the difficulties which have beset the work of the Highland
geologist.

At least from near Edzell in the north-east to Arran in the south-west, a
belt of slates runs parallel to and close beside, the Highland Border, flanked
on both sides by schistose grits. It was formerly thought that two grit groups
were present, with the slates lying between them as part of a straightforward
stratigraphical sequence. S. M. K. Henderson (1938) showed, by the use of
graded bedding in the grits as a 'way-up' indicator, that the slates were older
than the grits on either side and hence formed the core of an anticline—the
'Aberfoyle Anticline'. Although this is a complex fold, on a broad scale it is
essentially isoclinal and as no closure is clearly demonstrable the initial
evidence was equally compatible with its being (a) a true anticline (i.e.
upward closing) or (b) the downbent nose of a recumbent anticline, in which

case the fold would be downward-closing (i.e. synformal). J. G. C. Anderson (1947) considered that the anticline was upward-closing, but R. M. Shackleton (1958) showed, again by the use of graded bedding, that minor structures which are probably associated with the main fold are apparently inverted and 'face' downwards. For instance minor folds with cores of older rocks close downwards, not upwards as they should do in a normal stratigraphical sequence. They are therefore synforms, possibly representing inverted true anticlines. From such evidence he suggested that the Aberfoyle Anticline is likewise synformal being the nose of a recumbent anticline, probably of Early Caledonoid fold age, bent sharply down by the later Ben Ledi Antiform or equivalent arching folds (see above) and this view is widely accepted at present.

From the evidence of stratigraphical inversion as far south-east as the Aberfoyle area, Shackleton concluded that the close of the Tay Nappe could not lie in the Carrick Castle Fold (Bailey 1922) but must lie at least as far forward as the Highland Border area. It could well be represented in the Aberfoyle Anticline and this is the interpretation of the structure of the Southern Complex used in this handbook (see sections, Plate V, and Fig. 7).

## Notes On Fold History

In previous sections of this chapter reference has been made to Early Caledonoid folds, Transverse folds, and Late Caledonoid folds which, in each Complex, apparently represent successive fold phases of the Caledonian Orogeny. It may be that all folds of one style and orientation were formed simultaneously in both complexes but this is not certain in the present state of Highland structural knowledge. It is possible that there has been 'parallel evolution' in two successively-formed structural units which are represented by the Northern and Southern complexes: the triple division of 'early-transverse-late' seems to be a common one in orogenic belts.

It should also be emphasized that only the more important fold-systems which notably affect the distribution of strata have been described. It is possible that other folds may be found which are the result of local resolution of the main stresses. For instance King and Rast (1956) suggested a rather more complex fold development in the Cowal area than the triple one discussed in the foregoing account. G. Voll (1960) has also made a study of the structures of the South-west Highlands, and proposed a complex history of fold and cleavage development.

**REFERENCES**

Allison, A. 1933, 1940; Anderson, E. M. 1923; Anderson, J. G. C. 1935a, 1942, 1947, 1956; Bailey, E. B. 1910, 1913, 1914, 1917 (for 1916), 1922, 1925, 1928, 1930, 1934b, 1936, 1938, (*in* Bailey, E. B. and Maufe, H. B.) 1960; Bailey, E. B. and Holtedahl, O. 1938; Bailey, E. B. and McCallien, W. J. 1934, 1937; Bailey, E. B. and Macgregor, M. 1912; Barrow, G. 1904; Clough, C. T. 1897; Cummins, W. A. and Shackleton, R. M. 1955; Elles, Gertrude L. 1926, 1935; Elles, Gertrude L. and Tilley, C. E. 1930; Green, J. F. N. 1924, 1931; Gregory, J. W. 1910, 1931; Hardie, W. G. 1955; Harris, A. L. 1962, 1963; Henderson, S. M. K. 1938; Holtedahl, O. 1952; Johnstone, G. S. 1955; Johnstone, G. S. and Smith, D. I. 1965; Johnstone, G. S. and Wright, J. E. 1955; King, B. C. and Rast, N. 1956; McCallien, W. J. 1929, 1931, 1935, 1937; McIntyre, D. B. 1951; Pantin, H. M. 1961; Peach, B. N. and Horne, J. 1930; Phemister, T. C. and others 1960; Rast, N. 1958b; Rast, N. (*in* Johnson and Stewart) 1963; Rast, N. and Platt, J. I. 1957; Read, H. H. 1923, 1928, 1936, 1955; Read, H. H. and Farquhar, O. C. 1956; Roberts, J. L. and Treagus, J. E. 1964; Shackleton, R. M. 1958; Stone, M. 1957; Sturt, B. A. 1961; Suess, F. E. 1931; Sutton, J. and Watson, Janet 1955; Treagus, J. E. 1964; Vogt, T. 1930; Voll, G. 1960, 1964; Weiss, L. E. and McIntyre, D. B. 1957.

# 6. THE GRAMPIAN CALEDONIDES
## PART III: STRATIGRAPHY[1] AND LITHOLOGY

## ?Lewisian Assemblage

Rocks possibly belonging to the Lewisian Assemblage occupy a narrow strip of country, about 1¼ miles long and less than ¼ mile broad, lying in Glen Liath, near Foyers, which is on the south-east side of Loch Ness a few miles north-eastwards from Fort Augustus.

D. D. C. P. Mould (1946) has called attention to the fact that this 'Glen Liath Series' comprises coarse gneisses with associated limestones, intruded by basic hornblende-diorite and veins of pegmatites and granite, a facies which differs markedly from the neighbouring Moine Schists. All the rocks are crushed and sheared owing to proximity to the neighbouring Great Glen Fault and to the Glen Liath Fault which separates them from the Moinian strata. The rocks are never seen in unfaulted contact with the Moines and are unconformably overlain by Middle Old Red Sandstone.

Mould considered the possibility that the Glen Liath Series are (a) Moinian, (b) Dalradian, or (c) Lewisian and formed the opinion that they may belong to the Lewisian Assemblage. The evidence, however, does not appear to be conclusive.

## Moinian Assemblage

Rocks which have a close similarity to those found in the Moinian Assemblage of the Northern Highlands make up most of the north-central and north-eastern part of the metamorphic area of the Grampians. There is little doubt that they, too, are Moinian, and they are generally accepted as such. No stratigraphical succession has, as yet, been made out in them and they have been mapped on a lithological basis only, the one-inch maps showing psammitic granulite, pelitic schist, and 'undifferentiated schists'.

The chief lithological varieties are as follows. (1) *Psammitic Granulites* which are composed of quartz with varying amount of feldspar (potash-feldspar and acid plagioclase) and a small amount of mica, chiefly biotite. Such rocks represent metamorphosed sandstone. Occasionally, when lacking in feldspar, the psammitic rocks are represented by quartzites. (2) *Pelitic schists* (muscovite-biotite-schists) which represent metamorphosed shales and because of their metamorphic rank are often garnetiferous. (3) *Semi-pelitic granulites or schists*, which are intermediate in composition between the two varieties just noted. (4) *Striped schists* which comprise groups of rocks made up of (1) and (2) in alternate bands and laminae too thin to be individually mapped, the bands being an inch or so to several yards in thickness. Such schists probably represent a distinct depositional environment.

On the one-inch maps groups (3) and (4) were included with the psammite or the pelite bands as seemed most appropriate in each case. Psammitic

---

granulite is by far the dominant rock type making up huge areas of country of virtually uniform rock. Because of this the Moinian rocks of the Grampians are often referred to as the 'Central Highland Granulites' (Plates VI and VIIA).

Minor lithological varieties are also found. (1) Calc-silicate-granulites, which comprise quartz, feldspar and calc-silicate minerals such as zoisite, garnet and hornblende, occur as bands and lenticles within the main group-forming varieties listed above; although quantitatively insignificant, they are of widespread occurrence, and probably represent metamorphosed marls. (2) A remarkable aegirine-bearing granulite crops out in Glen Lui (one-inch Balmoral (65) Sheet); it has been suggested that this is derived from the weathering of an acid alkaline igneous rock but McLachlan (1951) considered that the aegirine is the product of potash metasomatism. (3) Limestones, which throughout the Moinian Assemblage of Scotland are extremely rare, are represented in the Grampian area by white marbles and greenish calc-silicate rocks, 20 to 25 ft thick, occurring near Kincraig House and again at Kyllachy House, Strathdearn (one-inch Grantown-on-Spey (74) Sheet); in both cases hornblende-schists are closely associated with the limestones. The true affinities of these rocks are problematical, and they may well form part of the Dalradian Assemblage as the term is here used. It is likely that some of the pelitic schists at present shown as Moinian on the published maps are also Dalradian. As will be seen from the next section of this chapter, the usage of the name Dalradian has altered with the years.

The Moinian rocks are all thoroughly crystalline, but the psammitic types locally show evidence of their sedimentary origin by the presence of current-bedding and the remains of quartz and feldspar pebbles. In many places they have a deceptive general dip resulting from isoclinal folding and this may be universal, but even allowing for the folding they must be of great thickness. J. Phemister (1960) suggested that similar Moinian strata in the Northern Highlands are of estuarine or lagoonal facies and tabulated arguments for and against Moine/Torridonian correlation. J. Watson gives a useful summary of the similarities and dissimilarities which have to be taken into account if the correlation of Moinian with various Torridonian groups is attempted.

It has already been pointed out that no stratigraphical subdivision of the Grampian Moines has as yet been possible. The names 'Eilde Flags' and 'Struan Flags', which have been given to the members of the assemblage contiguous with the Dalradian rocks, are not stratigraphical terms but were originally intended as non-committal names for rocks which have subsequently been accepted as Moinian. From a consideration of overall stratigraphy, however, it seems likely that the vast expanse of Moinian granulites of the Grampians can be correlated with similar rocks lying in the Northern Highlands immediately west of the Great Glen. These latter rocks are thought to be structurally, and probably stratigraphically, high in the Moinian succession. This view agrees with the Moinian/Dalradian relationships referred to in Chapter 5.

## Dalradian Assemblage

### General Description and Discussion

The Dalradian Assemblage (Plate VI; Fig. 6) comprises innumerable varieties of metamorphic rock-types—quartzites and schistose grits, limestones and calc-silicate rocks, slates, phyllites, mica-schists, black schists, etc.

all of which suggest a marine rather than the estuarine environment of the Grampian Moines. The earlier part of the Dalradian sequence is probably of shallow-water, possibly shelf-sea, origin, this suggestion being based on the presence of current-bedded (?shallow water) quartzites, limestones and pelites. The later part of the sequence may well be of deep-water origin. It is characterized by thick beds of slate and schistose grit in which graded-bedding is well preserved. In several areas these rocks could respectively represent

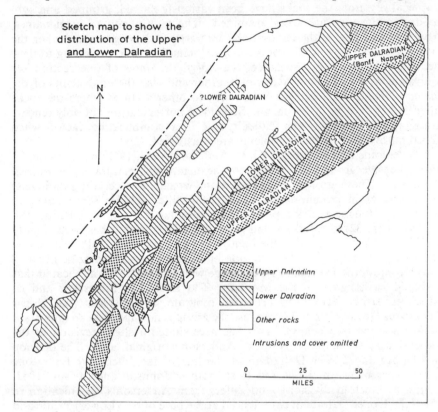

FIG. 6. *Sketch map to show the distribution of the 'Upper' and 'Lower' Dalradian, as the terms are used in this handbook (see Table II)*

shales and greywackes of a deep-water turbidite facies. They are associated with spilitic (pillow) lavas which may also have been erupted on a deep sea-floor, representing the ophiolites of a eugeosyncline.

It has been mentioned (p. 13) that the Dalradian, like the Moinian, is not a geological System but an 'Assemblage'. The Grampian Dalradian, however, is generally accepted as being, in large measure, made up of Cambrian strata, with the possibility that the earlier part of the assemblage may be late Pre-Cambrian or the equivalent of the Scandinavian Sparagmite formation. The only strata containing fossils of undoubted zonal significance generally included with the Dalradian are found in the limestones of the Upper Psammitic Group (see p. 39) which are of late Lower Cambrian age. What has been taken (with reservations) as scolithid tubes similar to the 'worm-pipes' of the basal Lower Cambrian of the North-west Highlands have been recorded from the Quartzitic Group of Islay (see p. 36). If the identification is valid, it would not greatly modify the suggestion of Holtedahl (e.g. 1952) and Anderson (1953) that the Dalradian rocks from the Quartzitic Group downwards are the equivalents of the upper part of the Sparagmitian of Norway.

Successions of Dalradian strata have been made out in several districts of the Grampian Highlands where, in common with most fields of stratigraphical research, the rocks have been variously named, grouped and subdivided in the separate areas examined. The multiplicity of local names, inevitable as details of the stratigraphy are unravelled, is aggravated when the rocks have been given different lithological names as well, according to their metamorphic state. For instance, the *Aberfoyle Slates* of one section are equivalent to the *Dunkeld Slates* of another and also the equivalents of the *Dunoon Phyllites* or *Pitlochry Schists* in two other sections where the rocks differ in degree of metamorphism. Such local nomenclature not only renders stratigraphical comparisons difficult, but is a complicating factor when structural or metamorphic problems are considered.

To overcome this difficulty J. G. C. Anderson (1948, 1953) has suggested a comprehensive 'group' terminology for the metamorphic strata of the Scottish Highlands. These groups comprise strata which have certain lithological characteristics in common and each group title includes some adjective indicative of the main rock-type or types, present, e.g. Psammitic, Pelitic, etc.

Table II (p. 32) is based on that given by Anderson, but has been slightly modified from the original in the light of recent work and Geological Survey classifications, notably in the retention of the Pelitic and Quartzitic (Transition) Group in the Dalradian Assemblage whereas Anderson advocated that it should be assigned to the Moinian. The Loch Tay Limestone and its associated strata have been accorded separate group status (the Upper Calcareous Group—see p. 38) because the group is now taken as an important marker horizon (see below). This has necessitated a slight revision of the nomenclature of the other groups of Anderson's original table. The division into Upper and Lower Dalradian at the line of the Loch Tay Limestone follows current usage (Knill and Rast, both *in* Johnson and Stewart 1963, suggest a threefold division), and differs from Anderson's classification in which the Upper Dalradian commenced at the base of the (Lower) Pelitic and Calcareous Group (Group 5). Many of the correlations of the more homogeneous groups have of course long been accepted and the overall equivalence of several of the more diversified parts of the sequences also generally recognized. Anderson's grouping of the latter rocks is, however, useful and greatly facilitates comparisons between the various sections through the Grampians.

Each sequence is reasonably well established by sedimentary structures which provide 'way-up' criteria, although these are only found in certain groups and then only when not obliterated by metamorphic processes. The successions and correlations are thus in agreement with the structural hypotheses given in Chapter 5. Indeed it must be emphasized that structural and stratigraphical hypotheses are interdependent. Many of the sequences have been subdivided even further than has been shown on the table, which, however, contains most of the names in common use. Expanded sequences are given, in several instances, under 'Lithology and Stratigraphy, (see below) but for complete stratigraphical details of each sequence the reader is referred to the works listed in the References at the end of this chapter.

One major assumption has been made in Table II, as Anderson pointed out in his original account. The rocks of Ballachulish and Lochaber (Ballappel area) have been directly correlated with those of the Southern Grampians Complex although everywhere separated from them by a slide. As will be seen from the table the Ballappel rocks fit well into Anderson's general grouping but some workers consider that they could belong to a separate trough of accumulation from that in which the Southern Grampians rocks were deposited.[1]

A lesser assumption in Table II concerns the rocks of the Banff area above the level of the Boyne Limestone. If the displacement on the Boyne Lag is considerable then the rocks above the Lag might not form part of the upper limb of the Tay Nappe as they have been taken to do in Chapter 5, and so might not correlate with the other sequences in Table II. Certain differences are pointed out on p. 38, but even if strict correlation is not possible, there is little doubt that the rocks are Upper Dalradian.

Figure 7 (p. 33) is intended to show synoptically how the stratigraphy of the various sections across the Southern Grampians Complex given in Table II can be correlated and how, within any given sequence, the alternatively named strata (bracketed in the table) are related. The structure is of course exaggerated and should be compared with Plate V where the sections, although somewhat diagrammatized, are less distorted.

## Lithology and Stratigraphy

### Group 1. *Pelitic and Quartzitic (Transition) Group*

The type area for the Pelitic and Quartzitic Group is Lochaber (Sequence A on Table II) where it is represented by an alternating series of pelites and current-bedded quartzites (commonly remarkably pure) sometimes referred to as the *Lochaber Series*. North-eastwards from this type area Anderson (1956) considered that the marked alternation of strata fails in the Monadhliath–Kinlochlaggan area (Sequence B). He suggested that there the Monadhliath Schists are the stratigraphical equivalents of several pelites and quartzites of Lochaber and are interbedded with the Eilde Quartzite and the (Moinian) Eilde Flags. An extrapolation from Bailey's classic paper on the Lochaber area (1934) indicates that the sequence might be attenuated by a slide (the Fort William Lag) as the Monadhliath area is approached, thus accounting for the missing quartzites. In this case the Monadhliath Schists could be in tectonic contact with the Moine rocks. This view cannot altogether be discounted but Anderson's evidence for interbedding is satisfactory and, if accepted, implies the lateral variation he has suggested. It also implies that Moinian and Dalradian strata form a continuous sedimentary sequence in the 'Ballappel' area by way of the Transition Group and this implication holds good whether the group be taken as Moinian (Anderson) or Dalradian, as is done in this account. Bailey (1934b, p. 499) has described a possible passage from Eilde Flags to the Lochaber Series in the ground east of Kinlochleven.

If the correlation between the rocks of the Ballachulish and Appin nappes with those of the Southern Grampians Nappe Complex, as given in Table II,

---

[1] See Note on p. 17.

## TABLE II
### SUCCESSIONS OF THE METAMORPHIC ROCKS OF THE GRAMPIAN HIGHLANDS
(adapted from J. G. C Anderson, 1948, table ii)

*Numbers and letters in brackets form the Key to Fig. 7*

**Classification**

| Classification used in text | Anderson, 1948 | Rast, Knill, 1963 |
|---|---|---|
| UPPER DALRADIAN | Upper Dalradian | Upper Dalradian |
| LOWER DALRADIAN | Lower Dalradian | Middle Dalradian |
| | Moinian | Lower Dalradian |

**Successions**

| Group | (A) BALLACHULISH AND LOCHABER | (B) MONADHLIATH AND KINLOCHLAGGAN | (C) LOCH AWE AND ISLAY | (D) CENTRAL PERTHSHIRE | (E) COWAL | (F) BANFF AND N.E. GRAMPIANS |
|---|---|---|---|---|---|---|
| Upper Psammitic Group (9) | — | — | Loch Avich Slates and Grits (a) | Leny Grits (b) / Ben Ledi Grits (c) [also: Green Beds] | Bull Rock Grits (d) / Beinn Bhuela Grits (e) [also: Green Beds] | Macduff Slates; Whitehills Group (g) |
| Pelitic Group (8) | — | — | Tayvallich Slates and Lavas (a) | Aberfoyle Slates (b) / Pitlochry Schists (c) / [Dunkeld Slates] (d) | Dunoon Phyllites (e) / Glenstuan Schists (f) | |
| Upper Calcareous Group (7) | — | — | Tayvallich Limestone (a) | Loch Tay Limestone (b) | Loch Tay Limestone (b) | Boyne Limestone (c) |
| Lower Psammitic Group (6) | — | — | Crinan Grits and Quartzites (a) | Ben Lui Schists (b) | Ben Lui Schists (b) | ?Gneisses (of Cowbythe, Ellon, Donside, etc.) (c) |
| Pelitic and Calcareous Group (5) | — | — | Ardrishaig Phyllites and Shira Limestone (a) | [Farragon Beds etc.] / Ben Lawers Schists (b) | Ardrishaig Phyllites (a) | |
| Carbonaceous Group (4) | Cuil Bay Slates | — | Easdale Slates (a) | Ben Eagach Schists (b) | — | Portsoy Group (c) |
| Quartzite Group (3) | Appin Phyllites and Dolomite / Appin Quartzite / Appin Striped Quartzite | — | [Transition Group] Islay Quartzite Series (a) | Central Highland Quartzite Series (b) | — | Durn Hill Quartzite (c) |
| Lower Calcareous Group (2) | Ballachulish Slates / Ballachulish Limestone | Kinlochlaggan Limestone | Portaskaig Conglomerate (Boulder Bed) / Islay Limestone (b) | Schichallion Boulder Bed / Blair Atholl Series (b) | — | Sandend Black Schist and Limestone Group (c) |
| Pelitic and Quartzitic (Transition) Group (1) | 'Lochaber Series': Leven Schists / Glen Coe Quartzite / Binnein Schists / Binnein Quartzite / Eilde Schists / Eilde Quartzite | Kinlochlaggan Qtzite. / Monadhliath Schists / Eilde Quartzite | Mull of Oa Phyllites (b) / Moal an Fithich Quartzite (a) | ?Schists and Quartzites of Rannoch (Outlier, affinities uncertain) | — | Garron Point Gp. / Crathie Point Gp. / Findlater Flags / West Sands Gp. / Cullen Quartzite (b) |
| | Probable passage | Probable passage | SLIDE | SLIDE | | ? |
| | Eilde Flags (Moinian) | Eilde Flags (Moinian) | Lewisian and Torridonian | Struan Flags (Moinian) | | Moinian |

*No direct connexion between the 'Ballappel' and Southern Complex sequences*

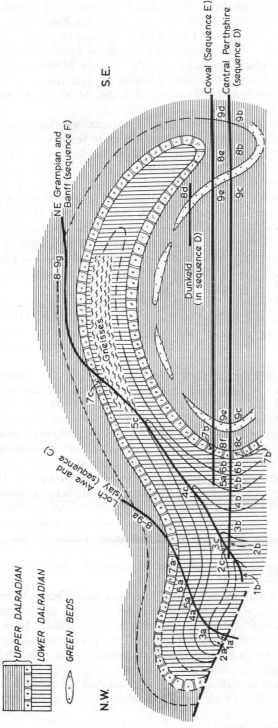

FIG. 7. *Derivation of the stratigraphical correlations within the Southern Grampians Nappe-complex*

This drawing is a highly diagrammatized representation of the broad-scale structure (compare sections, Plate V) and is only intended to show how the suggested correlations of Table II are arrived at, the key to the numbering being given on that Table. For instance within Group 7 of Table II, the limestone of sequence C (Loch Awe and Islay, 7a) is named the Tayvallich Limestone, while in sequence F (N.E. Grampians, 7c) it is the Boyne Limestone. In sequences D (Central Perthshire) and E (Cowal) the limestone has the same number (i.e. 7b), because in both areas it is known as the Loch Tay Limestone be accepted then the Islay succession of Group 1 (Sequence C) might well represent similar lateral variation away from the classic Lochaber area.

The Pelitic Schists and Quartzites of Rannoch (Sequence D) form isolated outcrops of what is possibly the Ballachulish Recumbent Syncline but other interpretations could be made depending on the validity of the structural correlation. For a description of the rocks the reader is referred to the Geological Survey Memoir describing Corrour and the Moor of Rannoch (Explanation of Sheet 54).

In the Banff area (Sequence F) the Cullen Quartzite was described by Read (1955) as a granulitic quartzite with subordinate mica-schists. It is, however, in places gritty and in this respect differs from the essentially even-grained Lochaber rocks. The West Sands Group is a mica-schist while the Findlater Flags are dominantly semi-pelitic rocks with some more siliceous ribs and occasional quartzites forming thin flaggy beds which pass into the calc-biotite flags making up the Crathie Point Group. The Garron Point Group comprises actinolite-schists and silvery mica-schists, differing from the Crathie Point Group mainly in the content of actinolite whose presence, of course, could be due to metamorphism rather than originally different composition; the two groups might therefore represent only one stratigraphical unit.

The Findlater Flags (also locally actinolite bearing) in several places strongly resemble the Leven Schists of Lochaber but it cannot be said that the Banffshire rocks show equivalence in stratigraphical detail to the Lochaber Series. Indeed, it would be surprising if they did, the two areas being 200 km apart.

Anderson (1948, 1953) referred the whole of the Pelite and Quartzite Transition Group to the Moinian Assemblage on the grounds that the first widespread marker horizon above the Central Highland Granulites is the Lower Calcareous Group (see below), the latter group of course indicating a major change from the psammite-pelite assemblages of the Moinian and the Lochaber Series. There are certain advantages in Anderson's classification, notably that unless his view is accepted, it would be difficult to assign certain pelite outcrops within the general area of the Grampian Moines to their correct Assemblage. The view is taken here that the lithological characters of the group are sufficiently different from the widespread Moinian facies to justify its retention in the Dalradian Assemblage, and so avoid confusion with published work and Geological Survey usage over many years.


*Group 2. Lower Calcareous Group*

The Lower Calcareous Group comprises limestone and other calcareous rocks together with pelites which are usually slates or dark carbonaceous schists. The development of limestone is different in the sequences from the various districts given in Table II and direct stratigraphical correlation of the various subdivisions of the group between the several area, has not, so far, been made. It is probably not possible.

In the Central Perthshire area (Sequence D), for instance, the group has for long been known as the *Blair Atholl Series* and comprises, in stratigraphical order:

Schichallion Boulder Bed—(see below)

White Limestone—(pale dolomite with some associated mica-schist)
Banded Group—(alternations of quartzite and schist)
Dark Limestone—(grey, with calc-silicate bands)
Dark Schist—(grey, slightly graphitic mica-schist)
These groups can be mapped individually over a wide area.

In the Lochaber area (Sequence A), however, the division is twofold, the Ballachulish Slates apparently forming a distinct upper horizon to the Group, while the lower horizon, the Ballachulish Limestone, is a limestone and calc-schist group within which thick, pure marbles form bands or lenticles.

In the Banff area (Sequence F) on the other hand the Sandend Black Schist and Limestone Group comprises at least seven marked limestone horizons, interbedded with dark schists and other rock types.

The Boulder Bed of the Lower Calcareous Group is of particular interest. Much of the 'Bed' consist of massive fine-grained psammite in which are set several distinct layers containing pebbles and boulders of exotic rock types, the most striking of which is 'nordmarkite'. In the lower part of the deposit the matrix rock is in places calcareous and there, too, the rocks are in some sections definitely bedded. Some boulders and pebbles appear to be tectonically deformed. The Boulder Bed is usually taken to represent a metamorphosed till, but in order to account for its wide distribution at a constant horizon it is considered to have been deposited from floating ice. It is not represented in the 'Ballappel' area.

## Group 3. *The Quartzitic Group*

Rocks ascribed to the Quartzitic Group form dissimilar sequences in the various sections given in Table II. All lie, however, between two characteristic horizons—the Lower Calcareous Group and the Carbonaceous Group. The rocks are notable for their high proportion of quartzites and the presence of bands of dolomitic limestone. In some sections the quartzite and pelite fractions are well defined and thus the group consists of one or two major quartzite and pelite horizons: in other areas many alternations of these and other rock-types are found and, in these districts, the group may pass by way of 'Transition Groups' of banded rocks either into the underlying Lower Calcareous Group or into the overlying Carbonaceous Group. Where these passage groups are found, there is, of course, no real geological basis for preferring their allocation to one or other of the major groups and their inclusion within the present one is chiefly for convenience in description.

The Appin Phyllites (Sequence A) are mainly grey pelites, commonly with abundant intercalations of fine-grained quartzite. At Onich the Appin Limestone appears to lie in bands at the base of this group but elsewhere forms a discrete horizon. The limestone is usually dolomitic and is of variable purity, the purer bands, which may be up to 40 ft or so in thickness, being pale, cream, or pink in colour. The Appin Quartzite is normally divisible into an upper half of gritty false-bedded quartzite and a lower half in which alternations of black slate and quartzite form a passage group to the Ballachulish Slates.

For a full expanded succession of the rocks shown in Table II (Sequence C) as the Transition Group and the Islay Quartzite Series the reader is referred to Bailey (1917) and to previous editions of this handbook.

The Islay Quartzite Series comprises quartzites, a notable slate group (the

Jura Slates), a dolomitic group in which the dolomites are of variable purity, and conglomeratic beds some of which resemble the Portaskaig Conglomerate of the Lower Calcareous group of this sequence, although probably of different origin.

The Transition Group is a series of phyllites, slates and quartzites, the various beds having local names. In Scarba these several groups are probably comprised in one undivided sequence, to which the name Scarba Transition Group has been given.

In certain dolomitic beds, included with the Islay Quartzite Series, B. N. Peach (*in* Geological Survey memoir 'Islay etc.') recorded worm-pipes similar to these in the Cambrian 'Pipe Rock' of the North-west Highlands, while the dolomitic beds themselves are of comparable lithology to the dolomitic Fucoid Beds of the latter district. There is some doubt as to the identification of the structures as true worm-pipes, but if they are, then the Islay rocks may represent basal Cambrian strata. Hackman and Knill (1962) recorded the presence of calcareous algae in these rocks.

The Central Highland (or Perthshire) Quartzite Series (Sequence D) is less diversified than the Group 3 sequences already described. Its divisions are as follows:

| | | |
|---|---|---|
| | Carn Mairg Quartzite | (Pebbly Quartzite) |
| Central Highland Quartzite | Killiecrankie Schists | |
| | Schichallion Quartzite | Quartzite<br>Dolomitic Beds<br>Quartzite (with a<br>conglomeratic zone<br>near the top) |

The Schichallion Quartzites are greyish or whitish, with some current-bedding. The Dolomitic Beds in the type area are represented by their metamorphic equivalents, tremolitic limestone. Their presence in association with the quartzites of course, strengthens the correlation between Perthshire and Islay. The conglomerate, which contains granitic boulders, is also similar in horizon to the conglomerates of the Islay sequence and, like them, shows some resemblances to the Boulder Bed of the Lower Calcareous Group.

The Killiecrankie Schists are pelitic rocks with alternations of more or less quartzose beds and with some graphitic bands. In the type area the schists are of quite high metamorphic grade. The Carn Mairg Quartzite is in part coarse and pebbly and in part quartz-schist. Locally it is difficult to separate from the flanking strata. According to A. L. Harris (personal communication) graded bedding is often well-displayed in the Carn Mairg Quartzite and the presence of this could be an indication of a deeper water environment than has so far been evidenced by the Dalradian Assemblage.

The Durn Hill Quartzite (Sequence F) is not a single quartzite but rather is a group comprising quartzites (both flaggy and massive) with intercalations of quartz-schist and mica-schist. A thin calcareous horizon has been recorded —it would be rather stretching probability to suggest that it represents the dolomitic beds characteristic of the other areas.

*Group* 4. *The Carbonaceous Group*

The Carbonaceous Group of 'black schists' is widespread, and, over much

PLATE VII

A. Flaggy Moinian granulite

B. Contorted Dalradian schist

of Scotland has a characteristic lithology of black graphitic schists (usually pyritous) with intercalated bands of quartzite and some limestone. The presumed representative of the group in the Banff area is, however, of a somewhat different facies, comprising an assemblage of mica-schists, variably calcareous flags and limestones. Graphitic schists occur in discrete bands in the lower part of the sequence and occasional bands of dark schist are found at several horizons.

*Group 5. The Pelitic and Calcareous Group*

The Pelitic and Calcareous Group in sequences C, D and F of Table II are of closely similar original composition. The group consists basically of calcareous pelites, more or less striped with thin limestone or calc-quartzite ribs. At certain horizons the ribs may be very numerous indeed. Over much of their outcrop the rocks are in the greenschist metamorphic facies and are now represented by very characteristic soft, fissile, calc-sericite phyllites in which epidote forms a notable constituent. At higher grades of metamorphism they form biotite schists with hornblende as the calc-silicate mineral.

The uppermost part of the succession shows considerable variation. In the Tummel area B. A. Sturt (1961) noted a group of rocks comprising mica-schist, quartzites, 'green beds' and hornblende-schists lying between typical Ben Lawers and Ben Lui Schists. This is his 'Farragan Group'. Further south-west Johnstone and Smith (1965) noted a somewhat similar 'Transition Group' in the Killin–Glen Lyon area. These probably comprise the Sron Bheag Schists of G. L. Elles (1930) which she recognized at Ben Lawers and Dalmally. In the Loch Fyne area the discontinuous Shira Limestone is developed at this horizon while nearby the thick Erins Quartzite (a group of predominant quartzites with some calcareous bands and other schists) and the St. Catherines Graphite Schists (graphite-schists with limestone and calcareous siliceous schist) are also in the same stratigraphical position. It seems likely that this assemblage of rocks is stratigraphically distinct from the Ben Lawers and Ben Lui Schists.

In Banff (Sequence F) the group is probably represented by the Cowhythe Gneiss. This is essentially a pelitic or semipelitic schist with a few limy bands and more siliceous ribs. A streaky quartz-injection varies considerably in intensity and from place to place results in the rock having the typical lit-par-lit appearance of 'injection' gneiss. Feldspathized rocks of granitic aspect also occur, but for much of its outcrop the rock is not really gneissose.

*Group 6. The Lower Psammitic Group*

The Lower Psammitic Group comprises psammitic and pelitic schists with the psammitic portion generally dominant and in places clearly gritty. Occasional limestone bands are found in the group, a notable one in Perthshire lying almost midway in the succession. In the least metamorphosed area (Sequence C) the Crinan Grits are distinctly graded quartzo-feldspathic rocks which are commonly quite siliceous, with subordinate pelites associated with several limestone bands. The graded beds supply clear evidence that in this area the rocks are not inverted (see 6a, Fig. 7). Throughout most of the Grampians, however, the group lies in the Loch Tay Inversion (under limb of the Tay Nappe) where the rocks have been rendered highly schistose.

D

There the rocks are known as the Ben Lui Schists and essentially are quartz-mica- and mica-schists, the original gritty nature of the psammites not always being apparent. As much of the Ben Lui Schists lies within the garnet or higher zones of metamorphism, the group was for many years referred to as the 'Ben Lui Garnetiferous Mica-Schists'.

There are no clear representatives of the group on the Banffshire coast (Sequence F) and it is possible that it has been cut out along the line of the Boyne Lag. Disappearance of the grits by lateral variation must of course be considered as a possibility, in which case the Cowhythe 'Gneiss' might in part comprise equivalent rocks. Further inland the group perhaps forms part of the gneisses of the Ellon, Donside and Cromar areas.

Although graded grits (some possibly of turbidity-current origin) have been recorded in lower groups of the Dalradian (Carn Mairg Quartzite and Cullen Quartzite) they are not of widespread occurrence and are found in relatively pure quartzites. From the Lower Psammitic Group upwards the psammitic fraction of the rocks is characterized by the occurrence in all groups of graded grits of heterogeneous composition, which resemble greywackes of turbidite type. This probably indicates a general change in the depositional environment of the Dalradian rocks.

### Group 7. *The Upper Calcareous Group*

The Upper Calcareous Group is characterized by the presence of crystalline limestone in thick beds, locally separated by subordinate mica-schists or various types of calc-schists. The limestone is commonly accompanied by thick bands of hornblende-schist or epidiorite. Some, at least, of the hornblende-schists may be paraschists, derived from calcareous mudstones of appropriate chemical composition. In the Tayvallich area the limestone in certain places passes into a calcareous grit and is associated with slaty bands.

### Groups 8 and 9. *The Pelitic Group* (8) *and the Upper Psammitic Group* (9)

For many years the Pelitic and Upper Psammitic groups have been taken to represent separate stratigraphical units but as research proceeds it is becoming increasingly difficult to maintain the division. For instance Harris (1962), working at Callander, considered that the junction of the Pelitic and Psammitic groups is diachronous, and in Banffshire the equivalent rocks are not clearly grouped into a pelitic and psammitic group but are interbanded, with, if anything, dominantly pelitic· strata stratigraphically *overlying* dominantly psammitic. Nevertheless in the Loch Awe, Central Perthshire, and Cowal areas (Sequences C, D and E) despite a probable diachronous junction, the uppermost part of the sequence certainly consists mainly of grits, while the lower part consists mainly of slates.

The rocks of the Upper Psammitic and Pelitic groups comprise a variable assemblage of psephitic, psammitic and pelitic rocks, together with some limestones of limited thickness but considerable importance. In the less highly metamorphosed areas the coarser-grained sediments are grits of grey-wacke type, now cleaved, while the finer grained rocks are cleaved siltstones and slates. In the more highly metamorphosed parts of the Grampians the psammites are represented by quartzo-feldspathic schistose grits or psammitic schists while the pelites are represented by phyllites and mica-schists (Plate

VIIB). One other variety is noteworthy—the Green Beds. In their less altered state these rocks are grits or schists containing much epidote and chlorite, which may represent either detritus from basic igneous rocks or tuffaceous material. In higher grades of metamorphism they become hornblendic schists. For some time the Green Beds were regarded as marking the transition between the Pelitic and Upper Psammitic groups in areas C, D and E, but Johnstone and Smith (1965) have shown that in the Comrie area they lie within a group indistinguishable from the schistose grits of the Psammitic Group, there again emphasizing the difficulty of considering the pelitic and psammitic rocks as separate stratigraphical units.

In areas C, D and E the Upper Psammitic Group grits, characteristically, have graded bedding, a feature which provides useful way-up criteria by which to elucidate the complex structures in which the rocks are involved. Other sedimentary structures noted include load-casts, flute-casts, etc. and some current-bedding, the latter especially in the finer grained sediments associated with the slates. The extensive development of graded beds might be taken as evidence that the grits were deposited by turbidity currents, perhaps under deep, or moderately deep, water conditions. In the Banff area (F) fewer of the beds are graded and the grading, on the whole, is less sharply defined than that in the equivalent rocks of the other areas. Other sedimentation features are common, however, and in several places in the Banffshire district slump structures are well developed and, indeed, are often spectacular.

In the Highland Border area J. G. C. Anderson (1947) recognized certain subdivisions of the Upper Psammitic Group. These are: Upper Grits; Leny Limestone and Shales; Lower Grits.

The Upper Grits occur in Bute and Arran, the Leny Limestone and Shales are found in several separate occurrences, while the Lower Grits comprise the main grit outcrops of the Highland Border belt, i.e. the Leny or Ledi grits.

The Leny Limestone and Shales were found by Pringle (1940) to contain fossils (*Pagetia*) of late Lower Cambrian age (*see also* Stubblefield 1958 and *in* Brown and others 1965, p. 133). Anderson, following Clough, Pringle and others considered that there are no criteria, either stratigraphical or structural for separating them from the main Dalradian outcrop.

## REFERENCES

*?Lewisian Assemblage:* Mould, Daphne D. C. P. 1946.
*Moinian Assemblage:* Barrow, G. 1904; McLachlan, G. R. 1951; Phemister, J. 1960; Watson, Janet 1963.
*see also* Memoirs of the Geological Survey.
*Dalradian Assemblage:* The Memoirs of the Geological Survey are the main sources of stratigraphical and lithological information. Most of the papers listed in the Bibliography for Chapter 5 deal to a greater or lesser extent with the stratigraphy but the following list comprises a selection of those whose content is of especial stratigraphical interest, together with additional references not so far given.
Allison, A. 1933, 1940; Anderson, E. M. 1923; Anderson, J. G. C. 1935a, 1942, 1945a, 1947, 1948, 1953, 1956; Bailey, E. B. 1913, 1917 (for 1916), 1925, 1928, 1934b; Bailey, E. B. and McCallien, W. J. 1934, 1937; Bailey, E. B. and Macgregor, M. 1912; Brown and others 1965; Elles, Gertrude L. 1926, 1935; Elles, Gertrude L. and Tilley, C. E. 1930; Geikie, A. 1891; Gregory, J. W. 1931; Hackman, B. and Knill, J. L. 1962; Hardie, W. A. 1952; Harris, A. L. 1962; Henderson, S. M. K. 1938; Holtedahl, O. 1952; Johnstone, G. S. and Smith, D. I. 1965; Knill, J. L. 1959a, 1960a; Knill, J. L. (*in* Johnson and Stewart) 1963; McCallien, W. J. 1929, 1931, 1935; McIntyre, D. B. 1951; Pantin, H. M. 1961; Peach, B. N. and Horne, J. 1930; Pringle, J. 1940; Rast, N. 1958a; Rast, N. (*in* Johnson and Stewart) 1963; Read, H. H. 1928, 1936, 1955; Read, H. H. and Farquhar, O. C. 1956; Shackleton, R. M. 1958; Stone, M. 1957; Stubblefield, C. J. 1958; Sutton, J. and Watson, Janet 1955, 1956.

# 7. THE GRAMPIAN CALEDONIDES

## PART IV: METAMORPHISM

The original sediments of the Moinian and Dalradian Assemblages have been subjected to a regional metamorphism associated with the Caledonian Orogeny, the rocks having been recrystallized under conditions which, considered broadly, were those of dynamo-thermal metamorphism. Platy metamorphic minerals were developed with a preferred orientation parallel to planar surfaces in the rocks, such as bedding or the axial plane cleavage of folds, while acicular minerals commonly grew elongated parallel to the axes of the folds.

New schistosities developed in connexion with each of the fold episodes discussed in Chapter 5, the schistosity of a later episode in places obliterating or replacing that of an older. Where the rocks lay beyond the limits of thermal metamorphism (as in the case of part of the slate belts of the South-west Grampians and Banff) the metamorphism took the form of a strong dynamic-ally-imposed cleavage which may be of slaty or strain-slip type.

The schistosities and mineral changes are most easily seen in the pelitic rocks and so are best displayed in the Dalradian Assemblage. The dominantly psammitic Moines are rarely strongly schistose as the original mineral assemblage, when metamorphosed, does not usually provide a sufficiency of platy or acicular minerals. The quartz and feldspar of these rocks has a granular habit, with the result that the psammitic Moines are often referred to as 'granulites' (*see* p. 27). It should be clearly understood that they do not, however, belong to the 'granulite facies' of metamorphism.

Apart from any introduction of material by metasomatic action, mineral assemblage in the rocks resulting from metamorphic recrystallization depends upon the following factors: (1) the chemical composition of the original rock, (2) the temperature and (3) the pressure. In rocks of similar composition the variations of temperature and pressure (it is possible that water vapour pressure may be especially significant) lead to the formation of different assemblages of minerals which can be arranged in an order or orders of increasing metamorphic grade. On the other hand, rocks of different original compositions affected by the same temperature and pressure conditions give rise to different mineral assemblages. G. Barrow first drew attention to one aspect of this reaction to varying physical conditions when in 1893 he mapped out lines in the South-east Grampians marked by the *incoming* of certain index minerals in pelitic or argillaceous sediments (Fig. 8). The zones eventually established by Barrow (1912) for the South-east Grampians were: (1) Lowest Grade—*Zone of clastic Mica*, with a very limited development close to the Highland Boundary Fault, (2) *Zone of digested Mica*, (3) *Zone of Biotite*, (4) *Zone of Garnet* (Almandine), (5) *Zone of Staurolite*, (6) *Zone of Kyanite*, (7) *Zone of Sillimanite*. Later work by C. E. Tilley (1925) led to some modifications of Barrow's scheme. For Barrow's zones (1) and (2) above he substituted the *Chlorite* zone and with this modification the zones given above are generally regarded as being typical of the '*Barrovian Type*' metamorphism. Tilley continued the delineation of the metamorphic zones beyond the area of Barrow's researches and eventually with Gertrude L. Elles (1930), published a map showing their distribution in the South-west Grampians, including Islay and Jura. In the same general area, E. B. Bailey (1923), employing different indices from those of Barrow or Tilley mapped the following zones: (1) mica inconspicuous, (2) mica conspicuous and

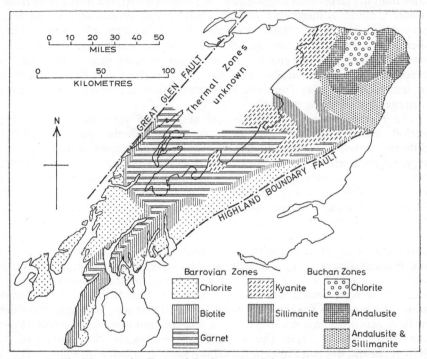

FIG. 8. *The Metamorphic Zones of the Grampian Caledonides* (*after Johnson* 1963, *following the work of several authors*)

(3) (a) mica with garnet, (b) mica with albite. In agreement with E. H. Cunningham-Craig, Bailey considered garnet as an alternative metamorphic product to albite, albite being produced under hydrothermal conditions of metamorphism (*see also* Bailey and McCallien 1934). Doris L. Reynolds (1942) and K. A. Jones (1961) considered that the albite is of metasomatic origin. M. P. Atherton (1964) suggested reasons why the biotite zone may be absent from the sequence, as is found in several places in the Grampians. In the north-eastern part of the Grampians H. H. Read (1923) and others have described a progressive metamorphism of pelitic rocks which gives rise to a type of metamorphism not found to the south. A central area of slate is there encircled by a belt of knotted slate and this passes gradually into schists in which the metamorphic mineral assemblage *andalusite–cordierite–sillimanite* characterizes the higher grades. This is the *Buchan Type* of metamorphism which has been studied by Chinner (1961), Johnson (1962) and others.

Barrow considered that the metamorphic zones were of the nature of gigantic aureoles round intrusions of the 'Older Granites' (see Chapter 8) and from this arose the idea that the metamorphism of the Grampians was monophase. For many years there was much discussion as to the time-relationships between this metamorphic episode and the folding. Bailey (1923), for example, regarded metamorphism and movement as practically contemporaneous, Elles and Tilley (1930) postulated widespread inversions of the metamorphic zones while Read (e.g. 1940) suggested that the metamorphism was later than the large-scale nappe-folds. It is now known that much of Barrow's 'Older Granite' is migmatite while the metamorphism has been found to be polyphase. In place of Barrow's concept of a 'metamorphic aureole' it is therefore more true to consider the metamorphism and migmatitization as resulting from the one process, in which an uprising migmatite front was preceeded by a metamorphic front with rock temperatures decreasing more or less regularly away from the migmatites, thus accounting for the zonal arrangement of index minerals.

The regional thermal effects waxed and waned throughout the folding period reaching overall peaks of intensity in different places at slightly differing times. The metamorphism was thus polyphase and the present regional zonal arrangement of minerals must therefore be the result of a 'high tide' (or the cumulative results of several 'high tides') of metamorphism. It has been suggested that the Barrovian Zones developed in regions where the rocks were metamorphosed under high confining pressures and the resultant thermal gradient was low, while the Buchan Zones were formed where the rocks were less highly loaded and the thermal gradient was steep. To some extent this is in agreement with the structural hypothesis given in Chapter 5, the Buchan Zones being characteristically developed in the Banff Nappe which is thought to lie at a high structural level where the rocks might be expected to have been under a lesser load than those of the Loch Tay Inversion—the type area for the Barrovian Zones. There are, however, difficulties in fully accepting this relatively simple explanation (*see*, for instance, Johnson 1963, pp. 140–141). The map, Fig. 8, shows the distribution of the Barrovian and Buchan Zones in the Grampians. It is based on Johnson (1963, fig. 1) following the published work of several authorities.

The mineralogical changes which can be observed in the Green Beds (see p. 39) as they are traced from south-west to north-east, i.e. from lower to higher zones, have been described by F. C. Phillips (1930). Typical members of the series are in order, beginning with the lowest grade: chlorite–albite–epidote-schist, biotite–epidote–albite-schist, epidote–biotite–hornblende-schist, garnet–biotite–hornblende-schist, garnet–hornblende-schist and hornblende-biotite–plagioclase-schist. Wiseman (1934) has studied the progressive metamorphism of epidiorites of the Older Igneous Suite of the Grampians.

The polyphase metamorphism referred to above has been described by Rast (1958a), Sturt and Harris (1961), Chinner (1962), Johnson (1962) and others, and a complex history of the relationship of folding to metamorphism has been worked out to replace the suggestions of Bailey, Elles and Tilley, and Read. According to the recent workers metamorphic mineral growth took place in some areas during periods of active folding and in others it took place during the 'static' interval between folding episodes. In general terms, however, Early Caledonoid folds were formed under conditions of low thermal metamorphism (in places such as the slate belt of the south-west Grampians possibly even beyond the limits of thermal effects). The peak of thermal metamorphism was reached in different areas either just before, during, or immediately after the Transverse folding and during this time the various index minerals developed in zones round the high-temperature regions. In some of these these latter areas migmatites were developed. During the Late Caledonoid folding, conditions of low thermal metamorphism once more obtained, at least over most of the Dalradian outcrop of the Grampians, with the result that the fold movements, in certain places, gave rise to retrograde metamorphism.

## REFERENCES

Anderson, E. M. 1952; Atherton, M. P. 1964; Bailey, E. B. 1923; Bailey, E. B. and McCallien, W. J. 1934; Barrow, G. 1893, 1904, 1912; Chinner, G. A. 1961, 1962; Cunningham-Craig, E. H. 1904; Elles, Gertrude L. and Tilley, C. E. 1930; Francis, G. H. 1956; Harker, A. 1932; Johnson, M. R. W. 1962, 1963; Jones, K. A. 1961; Kennedy, W. Q. 1948; King, B. C. and Rast, N. 1956; Kvale, A. 1953; Phemister, T. C. and others 1960; Phillips, F. C. 1930; Rast, N. 1958a; Read, H. H. 1923, 1927, 1940; Reynolds, Doris L. 1942; Sturt, B. A. and Harris, A. L. 1961; Tilley, C. E. 1925; Watson, Janet 1964; Williamson, D. H. 1953; Wiseman, J. D. H. 1934.

# 8. CALEDONIAN MAGMATISM

The igneous rocks associated with the Caledonian Orogeny have long been grouped into *The Older Igneous Rocks* comprising those 'earlier than or associated with the . . . metamorphism', and *The Newer Igneous Rocks* comprising those 'younger than the metamorphism . . ., but earlier than the Middle Old Red Sandstone' (*see* Read and MacGregor 1948). Following this division the 'Older' group included an early suite of basic rocks together with certain discrete masses of granite and the granitic fraction of what are now classed as syntectonic migmatites, the two latter making up the 'Older Granites' of G. Barrow (1893). The 'Newer' group comprised a suite of basic and acid plutonic, hypabyssal and volcanic rocks of which the earlier members were intruded in pre-Lower Old Red Sandstone, possibly Silurian, times while the later intrusions cut or involved strata of known Lower Old Red Sandstone age.

A more convenient grouping, and one which avoids any genetic implication concerning the origin of migmatites is:

(1) *The Older Igneous Rocks* (pre- or early-tectonic) comprising basic rocks extruded in the developing geosyncline, together with certain basic and granitic intrusions which either pre-date the general Caledonian folding or are associated with its early phases.

(2) *Syntectonic Migmatites* consisting mainly of composite gneisses which developed during the main movement phase of the orogeny and which were associated with the metamorphism.

(3) *The Newer Igneous Rocks* (late- to post-tectonic) comprising basic, acid and complex plutonic intrusions, minor intrusions and volcanic rocks. The earlier members of the group appear to have been involved to some extent in late Caledonian movements, the later members are completely post-tectonic.

De Sitter (1956) gave a simplified picture of the 'Orogenic Magmatic Cycle'—a sequence of magmatic and migmatitic rocks frequently found in orogenic belts of diverse location and age. This is:

*First phase*, basic rock intrusions (ophiolites) and extrusion of spilitic lavas in a geosynclinal stage.

*Second phase*, syntectonic migmatization accompanied by pegmatitic, granitic magma and late-tectonic granodioritic batholiths.

*Third phase*, post-tectonic volcanism.

It will be evident that the Caledonian igneous and magmatic rocks follow this general pattern fairly closely.

## The Older Igneous Rocks

### Contemporaneous Basic Igneous Rocks

Undoubted pillow-lavas were discovered by B. N. Peach in 1903 at Tayvallich in the Loch Awe district, being part of a great group of rocks of this

44

region that, up to that time, had been regarded as intrusions of a special type. These lavas are typical pillow-lavas of spilitic affinities, as shown by chemical analyses. By all except G. L. Elles they are said to present a bottom portion with pipe-amygdales, a central pillowy portion and a top vesicular portion, which can be used in determining the age-relations of the associated sediments. Tuffs and agglomerates are rare, but conglomerates containing lava fragments are common. Certain feldspathic beds in the Tayvallich peninsula are interpreted as crystal-tuffs.

In the River Blackwater, near Ardwell Inn, some ten miles south-west of Huntly (One-inch Huntley (86) Sheet), igneous rocks, probably basic pillow-lavas, have been described by W. Mackie (1908) and MacGregor and Roberts (1963). The position of these beds in the Highland sequence is not yet known precisely, but they appear to lie at approximately the same horizon as the Dalradian Tayvallich rocks.

**Intrusive Igneous Rocks**

The Intrusive Igneous Rocks may be subdivided into two groups: (i) Older Basic Intrusions, (ii) Older Granites.

*Older Basic Intrusions*

Older basic intrusions (shown on some old maps as 'greenstones') are well developed in the Dalradian Assemblage. They form sills or sheets often extending along the strike for great distances. Now almost everywhere composed of amphibolite, epidiorite or hornblende-schist, they exhibit their original character in certain favoured localities as at Portsoy in Banffshire, where the parent rock of the thicker sills is seen to be gabbro, with rarer enstatite–gabbro. The main horizon for basic sills is between the Loch Tay Limestone and the Central Highland Quartzite and a great sill, or sills, in this position stretches from Portsoy southwards for fifty miles to Deeside. At various points along this intrusion—Portsoy, Upper Deveron, Strath Don, Coyles of Muick—large bodies of ultrabasic rock, now serpentine and associated types, accompany the basic rocks. At Portsoy, also, the corresponding feldspathic pole is represented by a small body of anorthosite. Elsewhere in the Dalradian area thin sills are closely associated with the Loch Tay Limestone and, in Cowal, small bodies of serpentine are found. This 'Greenstone Horizon' has been employed by H. H. Read in certain correlations of the Deeside schists. The great basic laccolith on Ben Vrackie (Blair Athole (55) Sheet) in the Ben Lawers Group of sedimentary schists has produced hornfelses in the adjacent rocks which have thus been able to resist later deformation-movements, an observation confirmed by Pantin (1956). Some of the rocks mapped as early basic rocks in the north-east Grampians were considered by Stewart and Johnson (1960) to be sheared representatives of basic igneous rocks of a later suite (see below).

Associated with the lavas of the Loch Awe district are innumerable 'greenstone' intrusions not all markedly spilitic in affinities; with these occur rare soda-felsite, keratophyre and soda-granite-porphyry.

The progressive metamorphism of the epidiorites of the Central and South-west Highlands has been studied by J. D. H. Wiseman (1934).

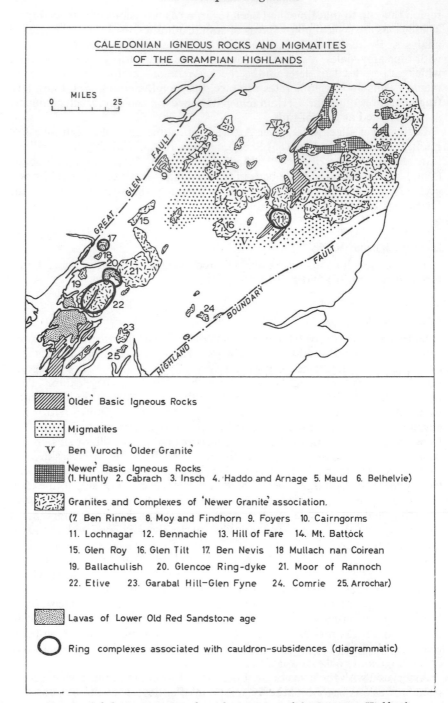

FIG. 9. *Caledonian igneous rocks and migmatites of the Grampian Highlands*

*Older Granites*

Certain granite masses within the Dalradian rocks are considered to have consolidated before the onset or during the early phases of the general folding. These are now represented by augen-granites such as these at Portsoy, Keith and Ben Vuroch. In the last-named area, six miles north-north-east of Pitlochry, a large granite intrusion has been investigated by G. Barrow (Geological Survey Memoir 'Blair Atholl, Pitlochry and Aberfeldy'). It has been profoundly affected by earth-movements resulting in the production of augen-gneisses. According to Barrow this movement came from the east-south-east, and on that side the intrusion has been sheared to a schist, while on the opposite side the rock has largely escaped shearing. Similarly, the country-rocks on the south and east sides of the granite have been greatly affected by the movement, whilst those on the other sides have been protected. These protected rocks show the hornfels or contact type of alteration. Other granite masses, some partly foliated, are found in Glen Clova and adjacent areas and have evidently been involved to some extent in the Caledonian Orogeny. While these rocks were included with Ben Vuroch in Barrow's 'Older Granites', W. T. Harry (1957) has shown that the Glen Clova group post-dates both the formation of the regional migmatites (see below) and the main metamorphism. It may be, therefore, that the Ben Vuroch and Glen Clova rocks respectively represent an early and a late phase of syntectonic granite emplacement although more information concerning the structural and metamorphic history of the Ben Vuroch area is needed before this suggestion can be confirmed.

## Syntectonic Migmatites

The classic researches into the metamorphism and igneous activity of the South-west Highlands were carried out by G. Barrow (1893) and he described, apart from Ben Vuroch, areas within which he identified various types of gneissose 'Older Granite'. This material rarely formed large masses but made up composite gneisses with the country-rock by permeation, veining, and the injection along foliation of 'lit-par-lit' threads. As the composite gneisses are followed to the south-east the amount of muscovite and microcline was thought by Barrow to increase, and that of biotite and plagioclase to decrease, a phenomenon which he explained as due to the straining-off of potash-rich material towards the south-east. The variation in the 'Older Granite' gneisses thus resulted from the progressive squeezing-out of the liquid portion of a granitic magma consolidating under stress.

From a more modern standpoint it is clear from the description of several areas of the composite gneisses (Read 1923, 1927, 1928, 1952; Williamson 1935; Reynolds 1942; Read and Farquhar 1952, 1956; Harry 1957) that they are essentially migmatitic in character. Their granitic fraction may therefore be of complex origin, resulting at least in part from syntexis and metasomatism. Barrow's hypothesis of 'filter-press action' to account for variation in composition is therefore outmoded and, indeed, Harry has shown that within the type area of Glen Clova it is incompatible with the evidence. Instead of showing the continuous variation suggested by Barrow the 'Older Granites' of Glen Clova, according to Harry, comprise two distinct phases— an early composite gneiss of migmatitic aspect whose granitic fraction is now represented by quartz–oligoclase–mica–gneiss and later discrete masses of intrusive microcline-granite. The migmatic rocks crop out in a wide semi-circular zone enclosing the North-east Grampians (Fig. 9) and show consider-able variation both in bulk composition (mainly depending on the host rock) and of the composition and nature of occurrence of the granitic fraction. The rocks may be porphyroblast schists in which isolated feldspars are more or less densely distributed in the host rock, or augen-schists or gneisses in which the granitic material occurs as small discrete lenticles, or lit-par-lit gneisses (sometimes referred to as injection gneiss) in which bands of more or less gneissose quartzo-feldspathic material alternate with bands of more or less altered host rock. In places the rocks are completely migmatitized to form granite-gneisses.

Reynolds (1942) considered that the migmatization followed the axial belt of the Tay Nappe and thus was possibly coeval with the formation of that fold. Read, on the other hand, suggested that the migmatite front rose through the nappe and thus the formation of the migmatites post-dated the Early Caledonoid folding. Sturt and Harris (1961) suggested that the migmatization began during the Transverse fold period (*see* p. 43) and continued after folding ceased, the resultant migmatites themselves being folded during the Late Caledonoid phase.

In south Aberdeenshire the gneisses probably represent migmatized rocks of the Ben Lawers and Ben Lui Schist groups (*see* Table II and Fig. 7).

In the Loch Laggan area, Inverness-shire, granitic pegmatites are locally so abundant as to form vein complexes (Anderson 1956). It is not yet clear whether these pegmatites are related to the migmatites, as seems to be the case for the large pegmatites of the area north of the Caledonian Canal, or whether they are more properly to be ascribed to the late- or post-tectonic magmatism. The full extent of these pegmatite areas is not yet known.

## The Newer Igneous Rocks

Great plutons and lesser intrusions cut the metamorphic strata of the Grampians and are clearly later than the main Caledonian folding and metamorphism, while the upper limit to their age is considered to be set by the Middle Old Red Sandstone which, in the north-eastern part of the area, lies unconformably on certain members of the group. Together with some volcanic rocks, these intrusions make up the suite known as the Newer Igneous Rocks. Because of lack of direct evidence provided by relationships to rocks of known age, and also the broad range of radiometric ages so far obtained, the date of emplacement of most of the Newer Igneous rocks cannot be stated within closer limits than these given above, but it is amply clear that they were not all formed at the same time.

One group certainly belongs to the Lower Old Red Sandstone, as in Argyllshire and southern Inverness-shire lavas are found which overlie, or are to some extent interbedded with, sedimentary rocks of that age, both lavas and sediments being cut by, or in places engulfed in, later plutonic intrusions associated with cauldron-subsidences. Rocks of this period are clearly post-tectonic, as none of the minor intrusions associated with the late plutons have been significantly folded. Some of the remainder of the Newer Igneous intrusions may also be of Lower Old Red Sandstone age. It is very probable, however, that many were emplaced, solidified and eroded before the deposition of the Lower Old Red Sandstone conglomerates of Argyllshire and the Midland Valley of Scotland immediately to the south-east of the Highland Boundary Fault, for these rocks contain abundant material whose only likely source is in the Grampian intrusions. H. H. Read (1961) has drawn attention to the fact that several of the granitic plutons, whose precise age is not known but which show the characters of 'forceful' emplacement, are likely to be pre-Lower Old Red Sandstone, contrasting them with the 'permitted' intrusions of the later cauldron-subsidences. The great masses of basic igneous rock found in the north-eastern part of the Grampians are earlier than some of these 'forceful' granites and there is some evidence that they have been involved in the last stages of the folding of the Early Caledonides (p. 50), this structural observation being in accord with their early radiometric-age dates. Some of the acid or intermediate minor intrusion which cut highly metamorphosed strata, are in certain areas, found to show signs of late-tectonic shearing or granulation.

Because of the uncertainty as to the date of emplacement of many of the masses it is difficult to describe the Newer Igneous Rocks by a treatment based on relative age. Any account, however, must deal separately with the characteristic group of late subsidence-plutons and dykes which cut the Lower Old Red Sandstone volcanic rocks and sediments, and, for the purposes of description the Newer Igneous Rocks will be divided into those 'mainly of pre-Lower Old Red Sandstone Age' and those of proved 'Lower Old Red Sandstone and Later' date.

## a. MAINLY OF PRE-LOWER OLD RED SANDSTONE AGE

### The Gabbros of North-east Scotland

In the Buchan and Strathbogie districts of Aberdeenshire and Banffshire there are half a dozen great sill-like masses of gabbroic rocks. These are of considerable size, the Insch Mass exceeding seventy square miles, the Huntly Mass fifty. The latter mass consists of sheet-intrusions of peridotite, olivine–gabbro, troctolite, and noritic gabbros and small granite bosses. The Insch Mass comprises peridotite, troctolite, olivine–norite, hypersthene–gabbro, quartz-diorite, syenite and granite. Other bodies show similar ultrabasic and basic types. The basic rocks are intruded by the more acid types. There is therefore in North-east Scotland a great petrographic province characterized by the development on a large scale of true calc-alkaline gabbroic rocks.

In many localities the original gabbro magma has reacted with sedimentary country-rocks of argillaceous composition to produce norites containing cordierite, garnet and other minerals not normal in pure igneous rocks. Such *contaminated igneous rocks* are crowded with innumerable small xenoliths of country-rock and their origin by assimilation of sedimentary material is beyond question. Good localities for studying such xenolithic complexes are at Cuternach at the eastern edge of the Huntly Mass, in the River Deveron below Castle Bridge at Huntly, at Easter Saphook at the east end of the Insch Mass, and especially at Wood of Schivas in the Haddo Mass.

Stewart (1947) and Shackleton (1948, also *in* Read and Farquhar 1956) suggested that the gabbros of north-east Scotland have been involved in the late stages of the Caledonian folding, thus accounting for their distribution and the steeply-inclined banding noted in several masses. Blundell and Read (1958) contested this view on the basis of palaeomagnetic observation, but Stewart and Johnson (1960) again maintained the folding hypothesis. There is growing evidence that similar major basic plutonic masses in the area north-west of the Caledonian Canal have been involved in the late folding and it is here suggested that the view that these basic plutons are later than the general metamorphism but earlier than, or contemporaneous with, the latest folding of the Grampian Caledonides, is likely to be correct.

(See also Ch. 9 for basic intrusions along the Highland Border.)

**The Granitic Plutons**

In the north-east Grampians the Granitic Plutons are represented by the great granite masses of Cairngorm, Lochnagar, Hill of Fare and Kincardine-shire, together with numerous small bodies, such as those of Bennachie, Peterhead, Strichen, Ben Rhinnes, Monadhliadh, etc. The form of some of these granite masses is thought to be laccolith-like, although Harry (1965) has shown that the Cairngorm mass, formerly taken as a typical example, is in fact stock-like. From this group also the granite of Lochnagar might possibly be excluded, as the shape of the outcrops resembles the ring structures similar to those found in the granites to be described in the next section.

The chief rock-type is biotite-granite with little or no muscovite or micro-cline, but these minerals become important in the Nairnshire granites (Moy, Ardclach), in some Banffshire examples (Strathbogie) and in the granites of Kemnay and Coull near Aberdeen. Associated with the large granite masses are small bodies of more basic character, consisting of hornblende–granites, tonalites and diorites; certain of these types are similar to members of the appinite suite of the South-west Highlands.

W. Q. Kennedy regarded the Foyers granite-complex as being the southern portion of the Morvern–Strontian granite-complex displaced sixty-five miles north-eastwards by the Great Glen Fault (Kennedy 1946, figs. 5 and 6; *see also* Mould 1946).

In the south-western Grampians the great granodiorite batholith of the Moor of Rannoch and the adjacent masses of Mulloch nan Coirean and Meall a'Chaoruinn may well be of pre-Lower Old Red Sandstone age although they are petrologically and probably genetically allied to the subsidence-plutons to be described later. The Moor of Rannoch pluton is cut by the Fault Intrusion of the Glen Coe subsidence and is thus clearly earlier than it, while H. H. Read (1961, p. 673) quoted it as a typical 'forceful' granite which has been eroded to supply material to the Lower Old Red Sandstone con-glomerates of Argyllshire. At its margin it forms an intricate intrusion com-plex or 'contact migmatite' with the surrounding country rocks. E. B. Bailey (1960, p. 187) believed that it could 'quite well belong to the Lower Old Red Sandstone suite'. It may be that these granitic plutons of the south-west Grampians represent remnants of the deep-seated magma-chambers into which the faulted blocks of the cauldron-subsidence areas settled.

**Basic to Acid Complexes**

Probably more or less coeval with the large, essentially granitic plutons of the Grampians there are numerous plutonic complexes, which range in composition from basic to acid. Amongst the more important are those of Comrie (mostly diorite), Glen Doll (serpentine, picrite, basic diorite, and diorite), Glen Tilt (augite–diorite, tonalite, hornblende–granite, biotite–granite, muscovite–granite, aplite) and of Netherly, Dandaleith, etc. Further south lie the group near the head of Loch Lomond—the complexes of Garabal Hill–Glen Fyne (peridotite, pyroxenite, hornblendite, gabbro, pyroxene–mica–diorite, appinite, quartz–diorite, granodiorite, aplite, and pegmatite), or Arrochar (pyroxenite, kentallenite, appinite, pyroxene–mica–diorite, hornblende–diorite, quartz–diorite, biotite–granite), and of Glen Falloch (picrite, kentallenite, pyroxene–diorite, appinite, hornblende–diorite).

In these basic-to-acid complexes the more acid types are generally the younger although not necessarily in the order set out above.

## Miscellaneous Rocks including Appinites

Throughout the South-west Highlands there are innumerable small bosses. Some of these are hornblendic rocks of variable, usually basic, syenite to diorite composition and they are probably petrogenetically allied to the more hornblendic varieties of the above mentioned complexes such as Garabal Hill. These hornblendic rocks make up the Appinite Suite. Other small intrusive masses are of augite–diorite, monzonite, kentallenite and cortlandtite.

In this area, too, several occurrences of appinitic explosion breccias have been recorded (Geological Survey Memoirs 'Colonsay and Oronsay', 'Ben Nevis and Glen Coe'; *also* Bowes and others 1961, 1963).

## Hypabyssal Suite

The hypabyssal suite is represented by a series of dykes, sills and small masses of calc-alkaline facies. Common types are: aplite, pegmatite, felsite, quartz–porphyry, feldspar–porphyry, microgranite, quartz–felsite, porphyrites with hornblende and biotite, vogesite, minettes, kersantites and spessartites, and peridotites. These are similar to the minor intrusions of Lower Old Red Sandstone age described below, but there are probably many series. Some at least appear to be older than the Moor of Rannoch pluton and the Etive and Nevis dyke-swarms (see below), and some have been found to show signs of having been metamorphosed after or during emplacement, although themselves cutting highly folded and metamorphosed rocks. (See also the reference to the foliated dykes of Colonsay, p. 12.)

## b. LOWER OLD RED SANDSTONE AND LATER

### Contemporaneous Igneous Rocks

Extrusive rocks, mostly lavas, belonging to the lower division of the Old Red Sandstone, form the Lorne Plateau, between Loch Awe and Oban and, in addition, appear in small areas in Glen Coe and Ben Nevis (Figs. 9 and 15).

*Lorne Plateau.* The Lower Old Red Sandstone igneous and pyroclastic suite of this district comprises basic andesites, hypersthene and biotite–andesites and felsitic lavas together with agglomerates, tuffs and tuffaceous grits. These rocks, together with associated Lower Old Red Sandstone sediments, rest with marked unconformity on the schists of the Grampian Highlands. The volcanic pile dips generally east-south-east and gradually thins in an easterly direction. The thickness of the volcanic rocks exceeds 2000 ft, whilst the local basal conglomerate varies from 100 to 200 ft. The general succession in Lorne in downward succession is:

5. Hypersthene–andesites, with intercalations of basic andesite and andesitic agglomerate.
4. Tuffs, felsitic flows, and hornblende– and mica–andesites.
3. Acid tuffs and basic flows.
2. Basic andesites with occasional flows of hypersthene–andesite.
1. Local breccias and conglomerates with shales and sandstone.

1. Subsidence , at surface —— Glencoe

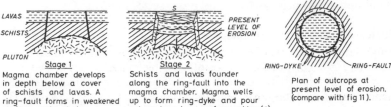

Stage 1
Magma chamber develops in depth below a cover of schists and lavas. A ring-fault forms in weakened surface rocks during a lowering of pressure in the magma chamber.

Stage 2
Schists and lavas founder along the ring-fault into the magma chamber. Magma wells up to form ring-dyke and pour out as lava in a surface caldera(s).

Plan of outcrops at present level of erosion. (compare with fig 11).

2. Subterranean Subsidences —— Etive and Ben Nevis complexes

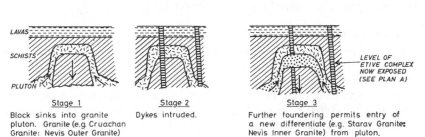

Stage 1
Block sinks into granite pluton. Granite (e.g. Cruachan Granite: Nevis Outer Granite) fills void left by foundered block.

Stage 2
Dykes intruded.

Stage 3
Further foundering permits entry of a new differentiate (e.g. Starav Granite: Nevis Inner Granite) from pluton.

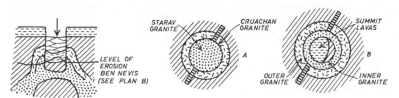

Stage 4 (Nevis only)
Surface lavas founder into the newly-formed subterranean cauldron.

Plans of ring-structures revealed at present level of erosion. A. Etive (compare with fig.12). B. Ben Nevis (compare with fig.13). Note that dykes do not cut later granites.

NOTE:- In stages 1 and 3 only two successive subsidences are shown for simplicity. The Outer Granite of Ben Nevis is itself composite, while in the Etive Complex four successive intrusions can be demonstrated. In Etive, also, a 'screen' of lavas is found between the two outer intrusions

FIG. 10. *Diagrammatic explanation of the mechanics of cauldron-subsidence*

PLATE VIII

A. The Glen Coe Cauldron-subsidence

B. The Glen Coe Boundary Fault

PLATE IX

A. Triassic Sandstone

B. Dolerite dykes of the Tertiary swarm

Rocks resembling ignimbrites have been found in the Pass of Brander district (*Sum. Prog. Geol. Surv.* for 1959, 1960).

*Glen Coe.* In Glen Coe (Fig. 11; Plate VIII) rocks of Lower Old Red Sandstone age occupy a cauldron-subsidence surrounded by an arcuate fault of some thousands of feet downthrow, against which the 'fault-intrusion' is chilled (p. 54). The rocks approach 4000 ft in thickness and consist entirely of basic andesites, hornblende–andesites and rhyolites, with quite subordinate breccias, conglomerates, sandstones, shales and grits. Erosion has revealed that, within the ring-fracture, this series rests with a marked unconformity on Dalradian and Moinian schists, its lowest member being a breccia.

*Ben Nevis.* The summit of Ben Nevis is formed by a core of volcanic rocks 2000 ft in thickness (Fig. 13; Frontispiece). These can locally be seen to rest unconformably on Dalradian schists, the succession being: basement conglomerate 8 ft thick, followed by 40 ft of black shale, and then agglomerates and lavas up to 2000 ft with a couple of bands of dark shale.

*Moray Firth Area.* Three outliers, hitherto mapped as Middle Old Red Sandstone contain a small development of volcanic rocks. It may be that these outliers should be grouped with the Lower Old Red Sandstone (p. 66), but if not, these igneous rocks might be regarded as the last members of the Caledonian suite in the Grampians.

*Mode of Eruption of the Lavas.* In Western Scotland both the Lower Old Red and the Tertiary volcanic provinces have dyke-swarms genetically connected with cauldron-subsidences. At the Etive Old Red Sandstone centre and at the Mull Tertiary centre the dyke-swarms cut the associated lava-plateaux. No instance of a dyke feeding a lava-flow has been recorded. The lavas in both provinces are therefore regarded by the Geological Survey as the products of central volcanoes, not of fissure eruptions. In both provinces sites of the smaller volcanic vents are inconspicuous. In the case of the Lower Old Red volcanic rocks there is confirmatory evidence of central eruptions. Very similar suites of lavas and tuffs are widely distributed in the Midland Valley of Scotland, but they are not there cut by dyke-swarms, and a number of scattered vents have been located.

In Western Scotland, as in the Midland Valley, the penetration of fine-grained sediment into cracks and cavities in the flows, and the intercalation of conglomerates, are characteristic features of the lavas. Pillow-structure is, however, unknown and the flows are not regarded as having consolidated under water. The lavas buried a hilly schist topography and are believed to have been erupted in a semi-arid terrain subject to periodic torrential floods.

## Plutonic Complexes

Two of the major plutonic complexes of the South-west Highlands—the Etive and Ben Nevis complexes—are shown to be at least of Lower Old Red Sandstone date by the presence within them of foundered masses of lavas of that age. These two plutons are thought to have been formed by the mechanism of cauldron-subsidence (see below) and closely allied to them is the subsidence area of Glen Coe which, although the only rock of plutonic association is a ring-dyke, is included in this section as an illustration of the mechanism involved. The rocks of these intrusions are mainly of calc-alkaline facies and almost all subdivisions of appropriate monzonitic or granodioritic types are represented by a component of one or other of the complexes.

E

*Glen Coe.* In the classic example of cauldron-subsidence of Glen Coe (Clough, Maufe and Bailey 1909; Bailey and Maufe 1916; Bailey 1960) a block of Lower Old Red Sandstone lavas and underlying schists subsided in a vast cylindrical mass determined by a ring fracture. As the mass (which

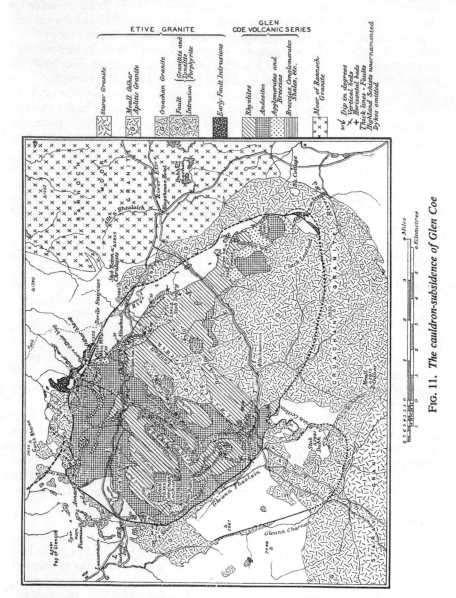

Fig. 11. *The cauldron-subsidence of Glen Coe*

originally measured some six miles in diameter) sank, so a 'Fault-Intrusion' (ring dyke) welled up through the fissure, in places chilling against the fault walls. This fault-intrusion at some places passes into the Cruachan Granite referred to below and at other places is cut by it: the intrusion consists of porphyrite merging into granite. This probably forms the simplest example of the phenomenon of cauldron-subsidence and is illustrated in diagrammatic form in Fig. 10. A more detailed map is given in Fig. 11. (See also Plate VIIIA and B.)

*The Etive Complex.* The greatest plutonic intrusion of the Lower Old Red Sandstone suite is that of the Glen Etive Complex. According to the views of

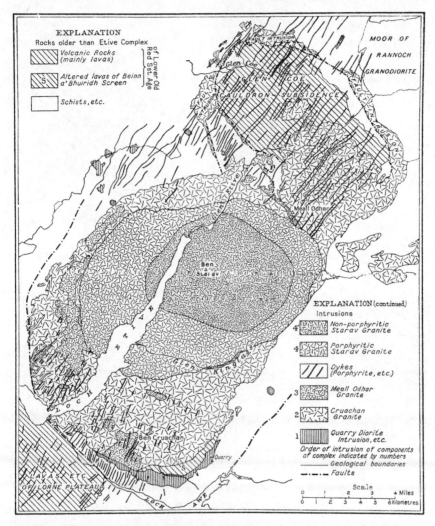

FIG. 12. *The Etive Complex and its relation to the Glen Coe cauldron-subsidence, partly after J. G. C. Anderson*

C. T. Clough, H. B. Maufe and E. B. Bailey (1909), as modified in detail by J. G. C. Anderson (1937a), it consists of a ring-complex of four, or possibly five, successive granitic intrusions emplaced as the result of four (or five) successive cauldron-subsidences. During each period of cauldron formation a somewhat cylindrical block is inferred to have subsided within a ring fracture, while granitic magma rose along the fracture-zone and occupied the space

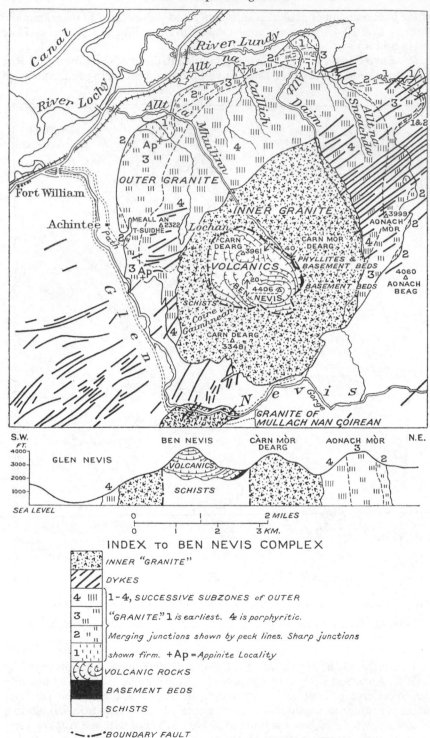

FIG. 13. *Geological map and section of Ben Nevis*

above. A remarkable feature is the presence of a 'screen' of lavas between the two outer members of the complex on its southern margin. The lavas have been thermally metamorphosed, and locally changed into schists by shearing during the subsidence. The method of emplacement is illustrated in Fig. 10 where only two successive subsidences are shown for simplicity. More detail is given on the map Fig. 12.

The Cruachan Granite has an advance guard to the north in the Fault-Intrusion (ring-dyke) of Glen Coe, mentioned above, which in some places passes into Cruachan Granite and in others is cut by it. It is likely therefore that the Cruachan Granite formed the magma chamber into which the Glen Coe mass foundered.

*Ben Nevis.* In the Ben Nevis cauldron-subsidence a somewhat similar mechanism has been inferred, there being a series of interrupted arcuate marginal quartz–diorite intrusions, an outer granite, and an inner, later, more acid granite (Maufe 1910; Anderson 1935b; Wright *in* Bailey 1960). The times of intrusion of the Inner and Outer granites were separated by a period of great hypabyssal activity. According to Maufe the circular mass of lavas forming the summit of Ben Nevis represents the collapsed roof of a subterranean cauldron already established during an earlier subsidence, the lavas and underlying schists sinking some 1500 ft into the Inner Granite while this was still liquid.

This structure is illustrated in Fig. 10, a detailed map being given in Fig. 13 (see also Frontispiece).

*Ballachulish.* The component rocks of the large granitic pluton of Balla-chulish (Lawrie *in* Bailey 1960) also exhibit a ring structure, but no lavas or large foundered masses are seen, but it could well have been formed by a mechanism similar to the Ben Nevis or Etive complexes. (See also the reference to the Lochnagar ring-complex on p. 50.)

### Hypabyssal Intrusions

Early intrusions of quartz–porphyry, felsite and hornblende–andesite in Glen Coe are probably contemporaneous with the volcanic episode of the district, but the later great swarms of north-north-easterly dykes are the main manifestation of the hypabyssal activity of probable Lower Old Red Sandstone age. The dykes were intruded during a period of tension after the intrusion of the first or outer granites of the cauldron-subsidences; few or none cut the later or inner granites (Figs. 10–13). Intrusions of this phase occur in vast numbers; it is estimated that of the long diameter of nine miles of the Glen Coe cauldron-subsidence, the elongation due to dykes amounts to two and a half miles. There are two main swarms or clusters of dykes, the Etive Swarm associated with the Etive Complex, and a lesser swarm at Ben Nevis. The petrographic types include felsites, quartz–porphyrites, biotite-porphyrites, hornblende–porphyrites, spessartites and olivine–kersantites. The order of intrusion of the different types of hypabyssal rocks is not uniform.

## Contact Metamorphism by the Newer Igneous Rocks

The contact metamorphism of the schists of the Grampian Caledonides by the Newer Igneous Rocks has received considerable attention.

Magnificent aureoles of thermal metamorphism are produced in the adjacent schists by many of the basic masses. The best example is seen at the northern margin of the Insch Mass, near Wishach Hill and Hill of Foudland. Here the upper surface of the gabbro is sloping gently to the north under a roof of slates belonging to the Macduff Group of the Dalradian Assemblage. In consequence, the breadth of the aureole of thermally-altered rocks is unusually great, being over a mile in some places. The unaltered slates are well-cleaved rocks, the cleavage coinciding with the bedding in most cases. The first evidence of contact-alteration is shown by the development of small rounded spots of andalusite and cordierite in the slaty groundmass: at the same time the rocks lose their cleavage and become massive. Farther in towards the igneous contact, the spotted rocks pass into totally reconstructed andalusite–cordierite–hornfelses of the inner zone of thermal alteration.

A. G. MacGregor (1929) and W. O. Williamson (1935) have described the hornfelses formed from the Glen Doll and Duchray Hill migmatitic gneisses by contact alteration associated with the Newer Granites. A. G. Hutchison (1933) has described the contact metamorphism of the Deeside Limestone, while in a classic paper C. E. Tilley (1924) described the effects within the aureole of the Comrie Diorite.

Around the plutonic intrusions of the Lower Old Red Sandstone group the country rocks have also been contact altered to produce hornfelses of composition appropriate to the original rock type. Notable calc-silicate hornfelses are produced from the Ballachulish Limestone. As these Lower Old Red Sandstone intrusions occur in districts where lavas and numerous dykes are found, good opportunities are provided for investigations into the production of hornfelses from these rocks. Andesite lavas and porphyrite dykes on contact metamorphism pass into granulitic rocks, brown hornblende and other ferromagnesian minerals giving place to small biotite flakes with aggregates of green hornblende and iron ores.

## Radiometric Age Determination

Much effort has been spent in recent years on the determination, by radiometric methods, of the dates of the folding and metamorphic episodes of the Scottish Highlands and, especially, of the various phases of Caledonian Magmatism. This study poses many problems and it is probably true to state that while the pattern which is emerging in general confirms the magmatic history set out above, much more information and refinement of method is needed before the full significance of the results obtained can be assessed. A useful summary of the information available is given by Sabine and Watson (1965).

### REFERENCES

*Older Igneous Rocks*: Allison, A. 1940; Bailey, E. B. 1913; Elles, Gertrude L. 1935; Harry, W. T. 1957; MacGregor, S. M. A. and Roberts, J. 1963; Mackie, W. 1908; Pantin, H. M. 1956; Read, H. H. 1928, 1961; Stewart, F. H. and Johnson, M. R. W. 1960. *Syntectonic Migmatites*: Anderson, J. G. C. 1956; Barrow, G. 1892, 1893, 1912; Harry, W. T. 1957; Kennedy, W. Q. 1946; Read, H. H. 1923, 1927, 1928, 1940, 1952, 1961; Read, H. H. and Farquhar, O. C. 1952, 1956; Reynolds, Doris L. 1942; Sturt, B. A. and Harris, A. L. 1961; Williamson, W. O. 1935. *Newer Igneous Rocks*: Anderson, J. G. C. 1935b and c, 1937a and b, 1956; Bailey, E. B. 1958; Bailey, E. B. and Maufe, H. B. 1960; Barrow, G. 1893, 1912; Bemmelen, R. W. van 1937; Blundell, D. T. and Read, H. H. 1958; Bowes, D. R. and Wright, E. A. 1961;

Bowes, D. R. and others 1963; Cameron, J. 1945; Clough, C. T., Maufe, H. B. and Bailey, E. B. 1909; Dakyns, J. R. and Teall, J. J. H. 1892; Deer, W. A. 1938a and b, 1950, 1953; Hardie, W. G. 1963; Harry, W. T. 1952, 1957, 1965; Hill, J. B. and Kynaston, H. 1900; Holgate, N. 1951; Hutchison, A. G. 1933; Hutton, C. O. 1938; Johnston, G. S. and Wright, J. E. 1957; Kennedy, W. Q. 1946; Lawrie, T. R. M. (*in* Bailey) 1960; MacGregor, A. G. 1929; MacGregor, A. G. and Kennedy, W. Q. 1932; Maufe, H. B. 1910; Mould, Daphne D. C. P. 1946; Nockolds, S. R. 1934, 1941, 1946; Nockolds, S. R. and Mitchell, R. L. 1948; Read, H. H. 1923, 1924, 1927, 1931, 1935, 1951, 1961; Read, H. H. and Farquhar, O. C. 1952, 1956; Reynolds, Doris L. 1936; Richey, J. E. 1939; Sabine, P. A. and Watson, Janet, 1965; Sadashivaiah, M. S. 1950, 1954a and b; Shackleton, R. M. 1948; Shackleton, R. M. (*in* Read and Farquhar) 1956; Sitter, L. U. de 1956; Stewart, F. H. 1947; Stewart, F. H. and Johnson, M. R. W. 1960; Tilley, C. E. 1924; Walker, F. and Davidson, C. F. 1935; Watt, W. R. 1914; Whittle, G. 1936; Williamson, W. O. 1935, 1936; Wright, J. E. (*in* Bailey) 1960; Wyllie, B. K. N. and Scott, A. 1913.
*See also* the Memoirs of the Geological Survey.

# 9. THE CAMBRO-ORDOVICIAN ROCKS
## OF THE HIGHLAND BORDER

Disconnected narrow wedges of rocks which, from their fossil contents, have been considered to range in age from Cambrian to Ordovician, appear at intervals along the Highland Boundary Fault (Fig. 14). These wedges are usually bounded by faults and the relationships of the rocks within them to the adjacent Dalradian strata to the north has been a matter of controversy.

For some years the rocks were thought to consist of a 'Highland Border Series' distinct from the Dalradian (or at least whose relationships to the Dalradian were unknown), comprising a group of grits, shales and limestones called the *Margie Series* and a group which mainly consisted of spilitic lavas, locally showing pillow structure, shales, jasper and chert—the *Black Shale and Chert Series*. The relative ages of the two groups was originally misinterpreted (see Barrow 1901; Pringle 1942; Anderson 1947) with the result that incorrect correlations were made between subdivisions of the rocks in the various discrete outcrops along the Highland Border.

According to Anderson, the original 'Margie Series' is in fact the equivalent of his Upper Grits together with the Leny Limestone and Shales (*see* p. 39) which he considered to be of the Dalradian Metamorphic Assemblage, and this correlation is widely accepted at present. If this view is taken then the remainder of the Cambro-Ordovician rocks of the Highland Border are largely made up of the *Black Shale and Chert Series* (whose affinities many take to be with the Arenig) together with an unconformable *Upper Series* (formerly confused with the 'Margie Series') comprising breccias, conglomerates, grits and limestone. The Upper Series Anderson took to be post-Arenig (?Caradoc); it is found at Aberfoyle and in Bute.

Associated with these sedimentary and volcanic rocks is a group of intrusive basic and ultrabasic rocks, represented by diabases, gabbros and serpentines, and their sheared derivatives, hornblendic and chloritic schists. Often the serpentine is represented by a thick dolomite belt. Patches of this serpentine appear at Scalpsie Bay and Loch Fad in Bute, Innellan and Toward Point on the Firth of Clyde, at Balmaha, Aberfoyle, Glen Isla, Prosen Water and elsewhere. Anderson considered that the ultrabasic rocks are associated with thrusting along an early development of the Highland Boundary Fault (see, however, p. 87).

As mentioned above, most of the outcrops of these Cambro-Ordovician strata lie in fault-determined slices, but in North Arran, Anderson and Pringle (1944) describe how rocks of the Black Shale and Chert Series lie 'disconformably' on Dalradian grits, the two apparently suffering the same degree of metamorphism (mainly cleavage). This apparently unfaulted contact is of considerable importance (see below). At Stonehaven Campbell (1913) showed that Downtonian strata (taken by him to be Silurian) unconformably overlie the Black Shale and Chert Series.

It has been pointed out that the Black Shale and Chert Series has been taken to be of Arenig age and it is generally agreed that there are considerable similarities between these rocks and Arenig strata of the Ballantrae district. From Aberfoyle Jehu and Campbell (1917) recorded the following fossils:

Radiolaria

Graptolitoidea

Brachiopoda: *Obolus, Lingulella* aff. *ferruginea* Salter, *L.* aff. *nicholsoni* Callaway, *Acrothele* (*Obolella*) *maculata* Salter, *A.* (*Redlichella*) *granulata* (Linn.), *A.* aff. *coriacea* (Linn.) *Acrotreta nicholsoni* Dav., *A. socialis* von Seebach, *A.* aff. *sabrinae* Callaway, *Siphonotreta* aff. *micula* M^cCoy, *S.* aff. *scotica* Dav., *?Schizambon.*

Phyllocarida: *Modiolocaris dakynsi* Peach.

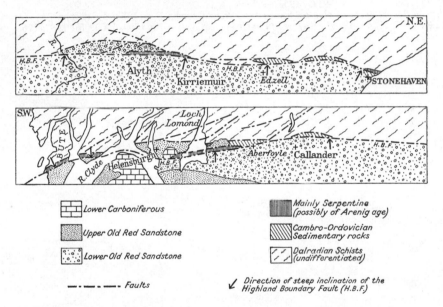

Fig. 14. *Sketch map of the Cambro-Ordovician rocks of the Highland Border and of the Highland Boundary Fault*
(For clarity the width of outcrops is much exaggerated)

These fossils were recently re-examined (*Sum. Prog. Geol. Surv.* for 1962, 1963, p. 57). Professor O. M. B. Bulman reported that none of the specimens figured as graptolites were acceptable as such while Dr. A. J. Rowell likewise found the brachiopod determinations unacceptable. The range of the fossils found could, according to the latter authority, be from Upper Cambrian to Ordovician (possibly even Lower Cambrian to Silurian) and hence the Arenig age of the rocks has not been proved by palaeontological evidence. This is of interest when taken in conjunction with the Dalradian/ Black Shale and Chert Series relationship found in North Arran.

The inference made from the Arran sections by Pringle and Anderson is that the 'metamorphism' of the Dalradian was post-Arenig and Anderson (1947) and Kennedy (1958) considered that the main Caledonian mountain-building (i.e. Early Caledonoid fold) movements in Scotland were likewise post-Arenig. The Black Shale and Chert Series is certainly cleaved in Arran and considerably folded in the North Esk (Edzell) area, but it no longer provides a firm datum, based on fossil evidence, from which to deduce the age of the folding. Until radiometric age determinations are carried out on the rocks of the Series, its postulated Arenig age depends solely on the comparison with the Ordovician strata of Ballantrae. In western Ireland Dewey (1961) has suggested a pre-Arenig age for the metamorphism, and hence for the major Caledonian movements.

## REFERENCES

Anderson, J. G. C. 1943, 1947; Anderson, J. G. C. and Pringle, J. 1944; Barrow, G. 1901; Campbell, R. 1913; Dewey, F. J. 1961; Dewey, F. J. and Phillips, W. E. A. 1963; George, T. N. 1960; Jehu, T. J. and Campbell, R. 1917; Johnson, M. R. W. and Harris, A. L. 1965; Kennedy, W. Q. 1958; Pringle, J. 1940, 1942.
*Annual Report of the Geological Survey* for 1893, Appendix E, p. 266; for 1895, p. 25; for 1896, p. 27. *Summary of Progress of the Geological Survey* for 1899, 1900; for 1962, 1963.

# 10. OLD RED SANDSTONE

The Old Red Sandstone formation of the region described here is divisible into three portions, Lower, Middle and Upper, each characterized by particular fish fauna. The Lower and Upper divisions occur south of the Grampians, whilst the Middle and Upper (possibly with some Lower) divisions, separated by unconformities, represent the formation to the north of these mountains.

## Lower Old Red Sandstone

The Lower Old Red Sandstone consists mainly of the lavas described in Ch. 8, which make up the Lorne Plateau between Loch Awe and Oban.

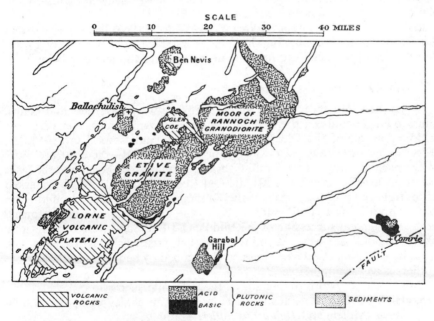

FIG. 15. *Sedimentary and volcanic rocks of Lower Old Red Sandstone age and their relationship to the Caledonian plutons of the South-west Grampians*

Sedimentary rocks are best seen near Oban and Kerrera (*see* Fig. 15) where they underlie the volcanic series. They evidently thin out to the east, where the lavas rest directly on the schists. The rocks comprise breccias, conglomerates, sandstones, grits, flags, shales and thin limestones. To the north of Oban, on Ardmucknish the basal conglomerates are most spectacular, some of the contained boulders being of large size, probably exceeding half-a-ton in weight, and are well rounded. The fact that many of these boulders are derived from lavas indicates that, although the main Lorne lava series overlies the sediments in this area, the conglomerates must have been derived from rocks erupted during an earlier phase of the volcanicity. It has been suggested that these early lavas formed volcanic islands in the basin in which the Lorne sediments were deposited and erosion of these islands provided the boulders of the conglomerates. Intercalated with the lavas are other thin sedimentary bands, in places associated with tuffs or boles (*see*, for instance, Ben Nevis, p. 53).

Fossils from the Oban area include the following[1]:

Plants:        Forms compared with *Psilophyton sp.* and *Pachytheca sp.*
Ostracods:   *Aparchites sp.*, *Isochilina sp.*, *Beyrichia?* or *Drepanella sp.*
Millipedes:  *Kampecaris forfarensis* Page, *K. obanensis* Peach.
Eurypterid:  *Pterygotus anglicus* Agassiz.
Fish:          *Cephalaspis lornensis* Traquair, *Mesacanthus mitchelli* Egerton and *Thelodus sp.*

In the Glencoe area a thin basal development of sediments is seen in places, underlying the lava pile. These rocks comprise breccias, conglomerates and red, green and black shales. In a band of black shales at the foot of Stob Dearg of the Buachaille Etive Mor group *Pachytheca fasciculata* Kidston and plant fragments have been recorded.

In the north-east Grampians area T. S. Westoll (1964) has suggested that the Rhynie Outlier, containing the famous Rhynie Chert, may be of Lower Old Red Sandstone age and not Middle, as hitherto thought (see below).

## Middle Old Red Sandstone

Along the south shore of the Moray Firth, between Inverness and Nairn, and around Fochabers, there occur extensive areas of rocks referred to the middle division of the Old Red Sandstone. Inland, several large outliers (Fig. 16), mostly preserved through faulting, are found—the chief are those of Drynachon Lodge, Tomintoul, Cabrach, Rhynie (see above) and the large Gamrie–Turriff outlier. The Middle Old Red Sandstone rests with marked unconformity upon the schists of the Grampian Caledonides; around Elgin and Nairn it is covered disconformably by the Upper Division of the formation. The general succession of the Middle Old Red Sandstone begins with a basal conglomerate which is followed by shales with fish-bearing beds, and these by sandstones and flags, but correlation bed by bed between the various outliers is as yet impossible.

The Inverness–Nairn outlier shows the following succession:

5. Hillhead Group, sandstones, flagstones and shales with *Millerosteus minor* (Miller) and *Homostius milleri* Traquair.
4. Inshes and Holm Burn Flagstone Group, sandy flagstones, dark calcareous flags and shales, micaceous sandstones and shales, with *Coccosteus cuspidatus*, *Osteolepis sp.* and plant remains.
3. Leanach and Dores sandstones with *Pterichthyodes milleri* (Agassiz), *Coccosteus cuspidatus*, *Homostius sp.* and *Glyptolepis sp.*
2. Shales and flagstones of Nairnside and Clava. From these have been obtained: *Dipterus valenciennesis* Sedgwick and Murchison, *Coccosteus cuspidatus* Miller and *Osteolepis sp.* at Easter Aultlugie, *C. cuspidatus*,

---

[1] Lists of fossils in this chapter have been compiled by Mr. P. J. Brand.

*Mesacanthus sp.* and *Cheirolepis sp.* at Clava Bridge and *Cheiracanthus murchisoni* Agassiz, *Cheirolepis trailli* Agassiz, *Coccosteus* cf. *cuspidatus* and *Diplacanthus striatus* Agassiz at Knockloam.

1. Basal Conglomerate.

The south-eastern portion of the Nairn outlier is celebrated for the classic fish-localities of Lethen, Lethen Bar and Clune, about six miles south-east of Nairn. The rapidly varying basal conglomerate is followed by thin sandstones, shales, calcareous nodules and thin seams of limestone, the latter making the fish-band at one time worked for lime. From these localities the following fishes were obtained: *Diplacanthus striatus, Rhadinacanthus longispinus* (Agassiz), *Mesacanthus pusillus* (Agassiz), *Cheiracanthus murchisoni, C. latus* Egerton, *Pterichthyodes milleri, P. productus* (Agassiz), *P. oblongus* (Agassiz), *Dipterus valenciennesis, Glyptolepis leptopterus* Agassiz, *Gyroptychius spp., Osteolepis macrolepidotus* Agassiz, *Coccosteus cuspidatus, Cheirolepis trailli* Agassiz and *Rhamphodopsis trispinatus* Watson. This fauna bears remarkable similarity to that of the Achanarras beds of the Caithness Flags of Caithness. The Hillhead Group of the preceding table is the highest horizon of the Middle Old Red Sandstone recognized on the south side of the Moray Firth, and corresponds to the Thurso Group of the Caithness succession.

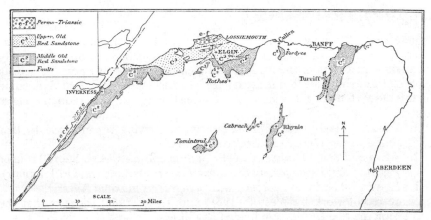

FIG. 16. *The Old Red Sandstone and Permo-Triassic north of the Grampians*

East of Elgin around Fochabers on the Spey, a considerable development of beds similar to those of Nairn is found resting unconformably on the metamorphic schists and covered unconformably by Upper Old Red Sandstone. Basal conglomerates are followed by shales and red sandstones with the Tynet Burn Fish-bed. This bed contains a fauna similar to that given above from the Lethen and Clune district. Still farther east is the great outlier of Gamrie–Turriff, faulted down on its western side into the schists. It consists of two divisions: (1) the Lower or Crovie Group of conglomerate followed by sandstones, flags and marls with ribs of limestone, and bright red sandstone; and (2) Upper or Findon Group, consisting of coarse conglomerates with a seam of red clay containing ichthyolites which have an assemblage of fish similar to the Achanarras fauna mentioned above.

In the valley of the River Bogie, south of Huntly, the Rhynie outlier is found limited on its western side by a large fault. This outlier is celebrated because of the beautifully preserved plant-remains in a silicified peat discovered by W. Mackie and described by R. Kidston and W. H. Lang. The succession from below upwards is (1) basal breccia and conglomerate, (2) lower red shales with calcareous band, (3) Tillybrachty sandstones with volcanic zone, (4) Quarry Hill Sandstone, and (5) Dryden Flags with which the plant-bearing Rhynie Chert is interbedded. The plants belong to the group Psilophytales, the chief genera being *Rhynia, Hornia,* and *Asteroxylon,* and the Myxophaceae (blue-green algae). Other fossils found in the Rhynie Chert include members of the insecta, arachnida and crustacea.

Volcanic rocks are developed on a small scale in three of the Moray Firth outliers, hitherto mapped as Middle Old Red Sandstone. A flow of vesicular andesite occurs in the Rhynie outlier, and another of similar nature in the adjacent Cabrach outlier. The former is associated in the field with an olivine-dolerite possibly of intrusive origin. A hornblende–andesite is found in the Gollachy Burn near Buckie in the Fochabers outlier and it is possible that this exposure represents rocks of Lower Old Red Sandstone age. An andesite sill cuts the metamorphic schists three and a half miles west-south-west of Cullen, in Banffshire.

## Upper Old Red Sandstone[1]

In a belt stretching from Nairn by Forres to Elgin and beyond, beds referable to the upper division of the Old Red Sandstone rest unconformably on various members of the Middle Old Red Sandstone or upon the schists of the Grampian Caledonides (Fig. 16). In the Upper Old Red Sandstone of this district three life-zones were established by R. H. Traquair. These are:

3. Rosebrae Beds with a fauna bearing a striking resemblance to that found in the Dura Den sandstones in Fife.
2. Alves and Scaat Craig Beds with *Bothriolepis alvesiensis* Stensiö (*major* Agassiz) and *Psammosteus megalopteryx* Trautschold (*taylori* Traquair).
1. Lowest or Nairn Sandstones with *Asterolepis maxima* Agassiz.

More recent work by Westoll (1951) and Tarlo (1961) suggests that the succession may be further subdivided as follows:

5. Rosebrae Beds
4. Scaat Craig Beds
3. Alves Beds
2. Boghole and Whitemire Beds
1. Nairn Beds.

In the Nairn area the Nairn Beds consist of grey and yellow calcareous cross-bedded sandstones with seams of clay and occasional flags and shales. They have yielded *Psammolepis undulata* (Agassiz), *Asterolepis maxima, Coccosteus magnus* Traquair, and *Holoptychius decoratus* (Eichwald). Further east in the Muckle Burn the lowest strata seen comprise a 15-ft thick breccia succeeded by sandstones with occasional conglomeratic, flaggy, and clayey bands. At Glenshiel these sandstones have yielded *Asterolepis maxima,*

---

[1] Notes compiled by Dr. J. D. Peacock.

whilst from two localities, Boghole and Whitemire, the following assemblages have been obtained, mainly by W. Taylor:

Whitemire: *Psammosteus megalopteryx, Cosmacanthus sp., Asterolepis maxima, Bothriolepis gigantea* Traquair, *Conchodus sp.* and *Holoptychius nobilissimus* Agassiz.

Boghole: *Psammosteus megalopteryx, Holoptychius nobilissimus, H. decoratus, Polyplocodus sp., Asterolepis sp., Coccosteus magnus* and *Eusthenopteron traquairi* Westoll.

This fauna shows a co-mingling of what Traquair regarded as typical Nairn and Alves forms.

In the Findhorn area the Upper Old Red Sandstone succession, which is faulted against Moine schists to the south (Black and Mackenzie 1957) begins with a reddish breccia followed by coarse cross-bedded yellow and reddish-grey sandstones with layers and galls of clay, and occasional beds of conglomerate which rest on the eroded irregular surfaces of the underlying sandstones. These are overlain by the Cothall Limestone, a concretionary limestone 10 ft thick, which is in turn succeeded by calcareous sandstones and marls. The following fishes were obtained by W. Taylor from the sandstone in the Findhorn section: *Psammosteus megalopteryx, Cosmacanthus sp., Asterolepis maxima, Bothriolepis major* Agassiz, *Holoptychius nobilissimus.*. This list is of interest in that it agains shows a mingling of forms characteristic of the Nairn and Alves beds. Westoll (1951) thought that these strata, together with those at Whitemore and Boghole might thus represent an important zone, and this suggestion is supported by a consideration of the distribution of psammosteid fish fauna (Tarlo 1961).

In the Elgin district the Alves Beds are composed of grey to reddish siliceous, pebbly sandstones which rest unconformably on Moinian rocks near Burgie, and the overlap of the lower part of the Upper Old Red Sandstone on other rocks appears to continue eastwards where the higher Scaat Craig Beds south of Longmorn (red and yellow sandstones and fine conglomerate) are separated from sandstone of the Middle group by a gap of only 200 yards. The beds at Scaat Craig and in the nearby stream have yielded *Psammosteus pustulatus* Traquair, *P. falcatus* Obruchev, *Cosmacanthus malcolmsoni* (Agassiz), *Bothriolepis sp., Conchodus ostreiformis* (M$^c$Coy), *Holoptychius nobilissimus, H. giganteus* (Agassiz), *H. decoratus* (Eichwald), and *Polyplocodus.*

The highest strata, the Rosebrae Beds, are exposed in Quarrywood near Elgin where they consist of brownish grey, yellow and reddish sandstones in which pebbles are scarce or absent. They have yielded *Bothriolepis alvesiensis, B. cristata* Traquair, *Phyllolepis concentrica* Agassiz, *Phaneropleuron andersoni* Huxley, *Glyptopomus elginensis* Jarvik, *Rhychodipterus elginensis* Säve-Soderbergh, and *Holoptychius nobilissimus.*

An important feature in the Elgin district is the change in thickness and character of the Upper Old Red Sandstone on either side of the probable northward continuation of a major fault which runs north-north-west through Rothes (*see* Fig. 16). On the east side of the fault a considerable thickness of strata including a cornstone group lies between the Rosebrae Beds and the Scaat Craig Beds but on the west side of the fault no representatives of either the Scaat Craig Beds or the cornstone group are seen. This evidence suggests that some movement of the fault may have taken place during Upper Old Red Sandstone times.

In a study of the heavy minerals of the sandstones of Elgin and adjacent districts, Mackie concluded that these minerals tend to be large and angular in the rocks of the Middle Old Red Sandstone but small and rounded in the Upper division. The assemblages of heavy minerals differ in the two divisions, particularly in the coarser sandstones, the Middle Old Red Sandstone showing dominant garnet with abundant iron ore, rutile, monazite, staurolite (locally), and some epidote, whereas the Upper division has zircon as its main heavy mineral with abundant tourmaline, rutile, anatase, and monazite.

Rocks referred on lithological grounds to the Upper Old Red Sandstone overlie Dalradian schists and Cambro-Ordovician rocks to the north-west of the Highland Boundary Fault in the Loch Lomond–Helensburgh area (Fig. 14).

## REFERENCES

The Memoirs of the Geological Survey are the main source of information concerning the Old Red Sandstone. *see also:*
*Lower Old Red Sandstone:* Westoll, T. S. 1964.
*Middle Old Red Sandstone:* Croft, W. N. and George, E. A. 1959; Geikie, A. 1879; Horne, J. 1901; Kidston, R. 1923; Kidston, R. and Lang, W. H. 1917; Lang, W. H. 1922; Mackie, W. 1914; Tarlo, L. B. 1961; Tasch, P. 1957; Traquair, R. H. 1896; Watson, D. M. S. 1908; Westoll, T. S. 1951, 1964.
*Upper Old Red Sandstone:* Black, G. P. and MacKenzie, D. H. 1957; Evans, J. W. (*in* Evans, J. W. and Stubblefield, C. J.) 1929; Horne, J. 1901; Kidston, R. and Lang, W. H. 1924; Mackie, W. 1897; Tarlo, L. B. 1961; Traquair, R. H. 1896, 1897; Westoll, T. S. 1937, 1951, 1964.

# II. CARBONIFEROUS

*Note; The Classification of the Scottish Carboniferous system has been revised (MacGregor 1960) since the date when Carboniferous rocks of the Grampian Highlands were last investigated in detail. It is not altogether clear how the original subdivisions in the latter area should be modified to integrate with the classification now employed in the rest of Scotland and, for the purposes of this handbook, the original nomenclature has been retained, with outmoded terms shown in inverted commas (see also Table I).*

North of the Highland Boundary Fault, rocks of Carboniferous age occur at four widely separated localities in Argyllshire and also are found in Dunbartonshire. The most northerly is at Inninmore Bay on the north shore of the Sound of Mull, where there is a small outlier of Upper Carboniferous sediment overlain by Triassic and Lower Liassic strata and underlain, probably directly, by Moinian rocks. This locality, being north of the Great Glen, is referred to in 'British Regional Geology: The Northern Highlands'. The other three Carboniferous outcrops of Argyllshire lie within the Grampian Highlands area; they occur: (1) at Bridge of Awe, towards the west end of the Pass of Brander, (2) on Glas Eilean, in the Sound of Islay, and (3) at Machrihanish in the Kintyre Peninsula. The largest of these outliers, which covers about twelve square miles between Machrihanish and Campbeltown, contains worked coals of the Limestone Coal Group. George (1960, pp. 76-7) considered that these Highland occurrences of Carboniferous rocks indicate the continuation of a cuvette of sedimentation which 'extended indefinitely northwards from . . . the Midland Valley trough', thus indicating that 'the Highland zone was not everywhere highland in Carboniferous times.'

*Bridge of Awe.* A few exposures on the banks of the River Awe, mainly above Bridge of Awe, indicate the occurrence of a small outlier of Carboniferous sediments, about one-fifth of a square mile in area, resting on Lower Old Red Sandstone lavas. The beds consist of 50 ft to 60 ft of gritty sandstones, mottled marls, and purplish shales, together with some lighter coloured shaly sandstones which have yielded a few poorly preserved plant remains. The Carboniferous age of the sediments is shown by the presence of plant species probably to be referred to the genus *Asterocalamites,* and of forms very like *Rhacopteris petiolata* (Goeppert). In 1899, Kidston expressed the opinion that the plants had 'a Calciferous Sandstone (Lower Carboniferous) facies' but the recent review of available evidence leaves their position in the Carboniferous succession still uncertain. Lithologically the Bridge of Awe beds have a resemblance to certain of the lower strata at Inninmore, twenty miles west-north-westwards on the Sound of Mull. W. Q. Kennedy has used the occurrence of Carboniferous rocks at these two localities as an argument in favour of assigning a Pre-'Upper Carboniferous' age to the main movement along the Great Glen Fault (1946).

F

*Glas Eilean*

On this islet, on the east side of the Sound of Islay and three miles south-south-east of Portaskaig, 20 ft or so of conglomerate, made up almost entirely of rounded or sub-angular pebbles of Jura Quartzite, are succeeded by a few feet of reddish-brown, fine-grained sandstone, followed by some 200 ft of volcanic rocks. These lavas comprise four flows of olivine–basalt, in which analcite has locally been recognized. Thin layers of sandstone are present on the slaggy tops of the two lowest flows; a 6-in fine-grained, sandy limestone, overlying the third flow, is regarded as a product of hot springs. As no associated fossils have been found, the age of the rocks depends mainly on

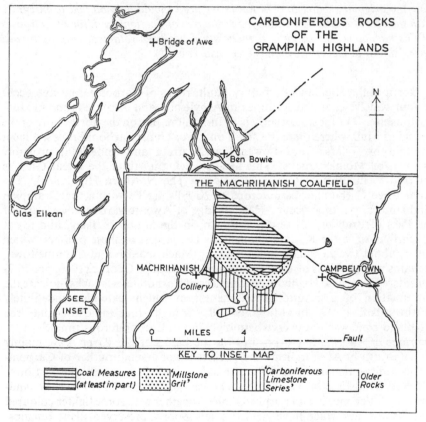

FIG. 17. *Carboniferous rocks of the Grampian Highlands*
(Inset map adapted from 'Report of the Scottish Coalfields Committee' *Scottish Home Dept.* 1944)

petrological evidence afforded by the lavas. These were originally assigned, without detailed microscopic examination, to the Lower Old Red Sandstone (*Sum. Prog. Geol. Surv.* 1898). An investigation by Pringle, A. G. MacGregor and Bailey, has led to the conclusion that they are Carboniferous: they may belong either to a 'Calciferous Sandstone' or to a 'Millstone Grit' Volcanic episode (Pringle 1944).

*Machrihanish*

The subdivisions of the Carboniferous of Machrihanish and Campbeltown range from 'Calciferous Sandstone Series' to Coal Measures (Fig. 17). The former consists of a thick development of volcanic rocks (olivine–basalts, trachyandesites, and trachytes: *see* McCallien 1928), overlain by some reddish clays of a bauxitic nature, formed as residual and detrital lateritic deposits derived from contemporaneously decomposing lavas (cf. MacGregor 1937, pp. 50–51). There are associated intrusions, mainly trachytic (ortho-phyre and keratophyre: *see* McCallien 1928). The 'Carboniferous Limestone Series' rests unconformably on the volcanic rocks. On the shore at Machri-hanish red limestone and limy shales assigned to the Lower Limestone Group succeed the red bauxitic clays above the lavas. There is some evidence to suggest that the succeeding Limestone Coal Group rests, with an easterly overlap, on an irregularly eroded floor of 'Calciferous Sandstone' volcanics and that, accordingly, the full succession is only present in the west. Nothing is known about the development of the Limestone Coal Group in the deeper northern part of the Machrihanish field, but in this direction the Main Coal, where not cut out by overlap, must lie at progressively greater depths. The Group is about 390 ft in thickness and contains a number of coal seams, one of which, the Main Coal, has been extensively wrought; old workings extend for some distance under the sea. The Main Coal, generally 10 ft to 12 ft thick, but of inferior quality near the top, was worked from the old Argyll Colliery; the workings were discontinued in 1925 owing to an outbreak of fire. Mines have, however, lately been driven to open out the coal in an untouched area. A thick sandstone forming the roof of this seam was also mined underground, principally as a source of moulding sand. A coal, about 110 ft above the Main, was at one time worked on a small scale; this Kilkivan Coal was last wrought for a short time between 1925 and 1927. The Lime-stone Coal Group is succeeded by the Upper Limestone Group, locally about 290 ft thick and containing three or four marine limestones[1]. Above this, the 'Millstone Grit' consists largely of basic lava flows of varying thickness with well defined boles of reddish mudstone. An intercalation of sediments above the lowest lava flow includes a fossiliferous band with remains of gastropods and ribbed brachiopods. Recent bores have shown a considerable thickness of Productive Coal Measures, including some coal seams of workable thick-ness. Non-marine lamellibranchs from these bores include shells representa-tative of the *Carbonicola communis*, the *Anthraconaia modiolaris* and the Lower *Anthracosia similis–Anthraconaia pulchra* zones. Dwarfed forms of *Lingula* and an incomplete *Spirifer* were recorded from the Queenslie Marine Band in the bores. Other bores indicate that above the beds definitely deter-mined as Productive Coal Measures there occurs a group of red sandstones and marls of which no description is available and the age of which is not known.

*Dunbartonshire*

In the Loch Lomond–Helensburgh area of Dunbartonshire 'Lower Car-boniferous' sediments and lavas overlie Upper Old Red Sandstone. On Ben

---

[1] The Upper Limestone Group according to W. Manson (Geological Survey N. Ireland Memoir 'Ballycastle', 1966, p. 82) probably overlaps the earlier Carboniferous formations southwards.

Bowie these rocks are faulted, along the line of the Highland Boundary Fault, against Lower Old Red Sandstone of the Midland Valley (*see* Fig. 14).

## REFERENCES

Dixon, J. S. 1905; George, T. N. 1960; Kennedy, W. Q. 1946; MacGregor, A. G. 1937, 1960; McCallien, W. J. 1928; McCallien, W. J. and Anderson, R. B. 1930; Manson, W. and Calver, M. A. 1957; Nicol, J. 1852; Pringle, J. 1944; Pringle, J. and Macgregor, M. 1940; Scottish Coalfields Committee 1944; Thomson, J. 1865; Trueman, A. E. 1954. *Summary of Progress of the Geological Survey for* 1898, 1899, 1951.

# 12. PERMIAN, TRIASSIC AND JURASSIC

## Permian and Triassic

### Islay and Kintyre

At Port nan Gallan, a mile east of the Mull of Oa at the south end of Islay, a breccia associated with a sea-stack of limestone and schist has been described by B. N. Peach (Geological Survey Memoir 'The Geology of Islay etc'.) as filling a swallow-hole, or underground cavern, in the Islay Limestone. The breccia consists of blocks of quartzite, limestone and schist set in a matrix of bright red sandstone composed of well-rounded grains of quartz; according to Peach it resembles the basement beds of the 'Trias' of Arran, Ballantrae and Loch Ryan. These basement beds in the Firth of Clyde area were subsequently assigned to the Permian, but Mykura (1965) suggested that the age of the lower part of the 'New Red Sandstone' of south-west Scotland is in doubt and that in certain areas the 'Permian' rocks may in fact belong to the Carboniferous System.

Twenty-five miles to the east, on the west coast of Kintyre, there are bright red false-bedded sandstones with intercalated bands of coarse breccia composed of vein-quartz, mica-schist, and quartzite. The sandstones have wind-rounded and polished quartz grains and contain faceted pebbles of dreikanter type. The outcrops fringe the coast for at least eight miles, between Bellochantuy and Glenbarr, and northwards of Glenacardoch Point to Killean. These beds were long ago allocated to the Upper Old Red Sandstone, but J. Pringle (1947), pointed out the evidence of their desert origin and claimed that the Islay and Kintyre occurrences are both of Permian age. This claim seems well founded, for specimens of the Kintyre sandstones are indistinguishable from the Permian desert sandstone of Mauchline in Ayrshire (but see also Mykura 1965).

### Moray Firth[1]

Permian and Triassic sandstones are exposed to the west and north of Elgin and on the coast between Burghead and Lossiemouth (Fig. 16; Plate IXA). The disposition of these strata in two areas is probably the result of faulting, but for the most part the structural relationships are obscured by superficial deposits. The following succession, with slight modifications, is based on Westoll (1951) and Watson and Hickling (1914):

4. 'Stotfield Cherty Rock'.
3. Sandstones of Lossiemouth, Spynie, and Findrassie.
2. Burghead Beds.
1. Sandstones of Cuttie's Hillock (Quarrywood) and Hopeman.

---

[1] Notes supplied by Dr. J. D. Peacock.

1. *Cuttie's Hillock Sandstone*: West of Elgin the Cuttie's Hillock Sandstone covers an area of about a third of a square mile on the upper part of Quarrywood Hill, where it reaches a thickness of about 150 ft, and an isolated strip occurs further west at the Knock of Alves. It is a fine- to coarse-grained, grey to yellow-brown rock, commonly laminated, and varies from soft to hard and siliceous. At the base there are a few feet of rather structureless sandstone with pebbles, some of which were shown by Mackie (1901) to be modified ventifacts. Support for the view that the sandstone is of aeolian origin is given by the large-scale dune-type cross-bedding and by the 'millet-seed' sand grains. The beds, which rest with slight unconformity on the Rosebrae Beds of the Upper Old Red Sandstone, have yielded a remarkable but restricted reptilian fauna (*Gordonia*, *Geikia*, and *Elginia*) and have been compared by Watson and Hickling (1914) with horizons at the extreme top of the Permian or the Permian–Triassic boundary in Russia and South Africa. The similar Hopeman Sandstone, covering an area of under 4 square miles on the coast between Cummingstown and Covesea, has so far yielded no identifiable fossils apart from footprints. It shows fine slump structures at a number of localities and is locally partly cemented by fluorspar and barytes.

2. *Burghead Beds*: The unfossiliferous Burghead Beds, best seen near the village of that name where they reach 200 ft in thickness, underlie the nearby Hill of Roseisle and are faulted against the Hopeman Sandstone to the north. They comprise siliceous and calcareous pebbly sandstone with occasional silty seams. Sections of similar rocks capped by marly sandstone are exposed in old quarries north of Elgin and below the Triassic sandstone at Lossiemouth. At Inverugie they are overlain by a few feet of sandy limestone and chert equated with the 'Stotfield Cherty Rock'.

3. *Lossiemouth Sandstones* etc.: The sandstones of Lossiemouth, Spynie, and Findrassie, probably less than 100 ft in thickness, mainly consist of hard, often siliceous fine- to coarse-grained rocks coloured white, yellow, and pink. The joints are commonly coated by fluorspar, barytes, and more rarely galena, and fluorspar at some places forms a small proportion of the cement. Cross-bedding like that in the Hopeman and Cuttie's Hillock sandstones can be seen at Lossiemouth and Spynie, and this together with the occurrence of 'millet-seed' sand grains and the very sparse assemblage of heavy minerals is again suggestive of aeolian deposition. They have yielded the reptiles *Leptopleuron* (*Telerpeton*) *elginense* (Mantell), *Hyperodapedon gordoni* Huxley, *Stenometopon taylori* Boulenger, *Stagonolepis robertsoni* Agassiz, *Erpetosuchus granti* E. T. Newton, *Ornithosuchus longidens* (Huxley), *Scleromochlus taylori* A. S. Woodward, *Brachyrhinodon taylori* von Huene, *Saltopus elginensis* von Huene. Von Huene (1908) correlated these beds with the Middle Triassic Lettenkohle of Germany, but recent work by A. D. Walker (1961; 1964) suggests that an Upper Triassic age is more probable.

4. *Stotfield Cherty Rock*: overlying the sandstones at Lossiemouth and Spynie are a few feet of sandy limestone and chert, the 'Stotfield Cherty Rock', which was correlated by Judd (1873) with the marly limestone and chert cropping out below the Jurassic on the Sutherland shore of the Moray Firth. It has clearly been formed by replacement of sandstone and has been likened by Watson and Hickling (1914) to silcrete. At Lossiemouth in particular it

has acted as host for veinlets and disseminations of galena, pyrite, quartz, and calcite.

## Jurassic

During the borehole progamme carried out for the Geological Survey in 1964 a short distance south-west of Lossiemouth, rocks were encountered which, from their fossil content and lithology, appear to be of Jurassic age. The strata consist of sandstones, clays and mudstones and represent an out-crop, the full extent of which is not yet proved, but which is probably bounded by a fault on the north side (*Ann. Rep. Inst. Geol. Sci.*, pt. 1, *Sum. Prog. Geol. Surv.* for 1965, 1966, p. 66).

**REFERENCES**

Boulenger, G. A. 1903; Huene, F. von 1908, 1910a and b; Huxley, T. H. 1859, 1867, 1869, 1875, 1877, 1887; Judd, J. W. 1873; Mackie, W. 1901, 1923; Mykura, W. 1965; Newton, E. T. 1893, 1894; Taylor, W. 1920; Walker, A. D. 1961, 1964; Watson, D. M. S. 1909; Watson, D. M. S. and Hickling, G. 1914; Westoll, T. S. 1948, 1951; Woodward, A. S. 1907.
*Geological Survey Memoir* 'The Geology of Islay, etc.'

# 13. LATE-CARBONIFEROUS AND
## POST-CARBONIFEROUS MINOR INTRUSIONS

### Permo-Carboniferous Quartz–Dolerite Dykes

In the South-west Highlands there are innumerable examples of east-and-west-trending quartz–dolerite dykes which cut the north-north-east suite of Lower Old Red Sandstone age and are themselves cut by the north-west Tertiary suite described later. These quartz–dolerite dykes are comparable with the quartz–dolerite dykes referred to Permo-Carboniferous age in the Midland Valley, of which some of the Highland dykes are clearly continuations. Good examples of these dykes are seen in Cowal—at Carrick, Lochgoilhead, Loch Restil, etc. The Lochgoilhead dyke is probably a member of the set that begins at Perth, seventy miles away. Less abundant representatives of the quartz–dolerite suite are found farther north in the Perthshire Highlands, Deeside and Buchan. In Buchan a dyke extends westwards from Peterhead for forty miles to Rothie Norman. The quartz–dolerites consist of basic plagioclase, ophitic augite, iron oxide and micropegmatitic mesostasis.

Some doubt has been thrown on the use of the term 'Permo–Carboniferous' for the age of these dykes and other related rocks, by the suggestion (*see* p. 73) that some at least of the 'Permian' strata of the Midland Valley should be referred to the Upper Carboniferous. It seems best to retain the name in the Highlands until a satisfactory new terminology is evolved for the type Lowland areas.

### Camptonite Suite of South-West Highlands

At various localities in the South-west Highlands such as Colonsay, Scarba and Loch Leven, there are found camptonite and monchiquite dykes whose age is a subject of discussion. These dykes follow the same north-westerly direction as the dykes of Tertiary age. They are later than both the minor intrusions of Lower Old Red Sandstone age and the Permo–Carboniferous quartz–dolerite dykes. They are cut by dykes of known Tertiary age, but have never been seen to cut Mesozoic sediments or Tertiary lavas. A. Harker grouped with these dykes others composed of crinanite and olivine–dolerite and considered the whole assemblage to be of Permian age. That the camptonite suite is late Carboniferous or Permian seems very probable as a result of the determination by W. D. Urry (1941) of the ages of two monchiquite dykes in Colonsay, by the helium method.

A small patch of breccia, with an intrusion of nepheline–basalt, occupies an explosion vent in Coire na Ba (see Sheet 53 on Fig. 18); this may be of Permian age.

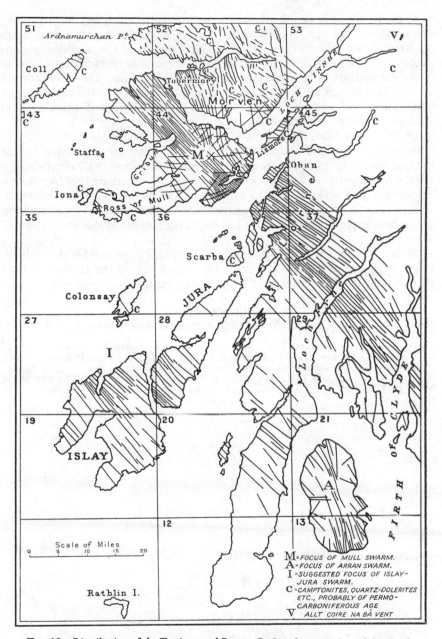

FIG. 18. *Distribution of the Tertiary and Permo-Carboniferous Dykes of the South-west Highlands and the location of the Tertiary Centres*
(The numbered rectangles mark the margins of the one-inch Geological maps)

# Tertiary Dykes, Etc.

In the South-west Highlands an immense number of dykes, mostly basic, run north-west or north-north-west. These dykes are grouped into what are apparently two swarms (Fig. 18; Plate IXB) one of which is evidently connected with the Mull centre of Tertiary igneous activity and another which on first sight appears to be connected with the Arran centre. The dykes consist of basalts, mugearites, crinanites, trachytes, teschenites, tholeiites, andesitic pitchstones and andesitic, trachytic and rhyolitic types. Composite and multiple examples are abundant.

Dykes of the Mull Swarm traverse Lorne and reach the Firth of Clyde. The southern group is now thought to consist, not of one single swarm centred on Arran, but of at least two swarms (McCallien 1932) comprising a true 'Arran Swarm' associated with more than one centre on that island, and an 'Islay–Jura Swarm' related to a centre which lies somewhere to the north-west of Islay. F. Walker (1961) suggested that the plutonic centre of this swarm is nowhere exposed at the surface but lies concealed under the north coast of the island.

Walker (1939) has also described an elongated boss on Maiden Island, Oban, which provides the only recorded occurrence, in the British Tertiary province, of the development of picrite marginal to olivine–dolerite.

## REFERENCES

*Permo-Carboniferous Quartz-Dolerite Dykes:* Geological Survey Memoirs *also* Buchan, S. 1932; Richey, J. E. 1939; Walker, F. 1935.
*Camptonite Suite:* Geological Survey Memoirs on the areas quoted and those on Mull and Caithness; *also* Harker, A. 1918; Richey, J. E. 1939; Urry, W. D. and Holmes, A. 1941.
*Tertiary Dykes:* Geological Survey Memoirs to the areas shown in Fig. 18; *also* Allison, A. 1936; Anderson, E. M. 1951; Bemmelen, R. W. van 1937; Harker, A. 1929; McCallien, W. J. 1932; Richey, J. E. 1939; Walker, F. 1939, 1961.

# 14. PLIOCENE(?), PLEISTOCENE AND RECENT

## Pliocene(?)

In the Buchan district of Aberdeenshire several small patches of gravels, composed mainly of quartzite pebbles, occur at elevations of 350 to 400 ft above O.D. These gravels contain flints with Cretaceous fossils and are overlain by the lowest boulder-clay of the district. It has been suggested by J. S. Flett and H. H. Read (1921) that these gravels are possibly of Pliocene age and indicate a submergence of this part of Scotland of at least 400 ft.

## Pre-Glacial Raised Beach of the West of Scotland

Throughout a small area in the west of Scotland there is a well-developed pre-Glacial shore-line at 100 to 135 ft above high-water-mark (Pl. XA). It occurs in Colonsay, Oronsay, Mull, Islay and Iona. Its inner margin is marked by a line of cliffs. It has been studied by W. B. Wright (1911), who tentatively correlated it with the pre-Glacial shore-line of south Britain.

## Glacial Period

The now generally accepted sequence of events during the Pleistocene period in the Northern Hemisphere includes at least four major glaciations. These were separated in time by interglacial periods, some of which were prolonged and during which the climate was at least as mild as it is at the present day. There is no clear evidence, however, concerning the glacial history of the Grampian Highlands before the last major glaciation, which in Continental European chronology is known as the 'Würm' or 'Weichsel' Glaciation.

The glaciation of the Grampians can therefore conveniently be considered in two parts. There was an early period of *Maximum Glaciation* of which little is known in detail except that at the end of it, ice had accumulated over Scotland to such an extent that all the land, with the exception of certain mountain-tops which behaved as nunataks, was buried under a continuous ice-sheet. In the Moray Firth area the presence of three superimposed glacial tills suggests that the development of this ice-sheet had a complex history but whether these deposits represent separate major glaciations of the European sequence or phases within the last one of these is not certain. Of the three stages indicated by these drifts, however, the last stage was separated from the other two by an interglacial or interstadial period. E. A. Fitzpatrick (1965) recorded a $C_{14}$ age of 28,000 years B.P. for material from an old soil buried under, or included in the drift associated with the last stage. This suggests that the last stage belongs to the later part of the period of the Weichsel glaciation of the European sequence.

During the maximum glaciation the Grampian Highlands were a great centre of ice-dispersal. The main distribution-centre seems to have been situated in the western half of the region. In particular the Moor of Rannoch was a great gathering ground from which ice flowed out more or less radially, except to the north where it was confluent with the glaciers originating in the Northern Highlands. The radial pattern was also modified by the interference of ice from subsidiary dispersal centres, such as the Cairngorm Massif, and by the influence of ice coming from outside Scotland. For instance on the east coast, glaciers flowing from the Grampians were diverted by the pressure of ice from Scandinavia while the south-westward flowing ice was deflected by glaciers originating in Northern Ireland causing it to turn to the west and north over the southern part of the Inner Hebrides. The movement of ice was

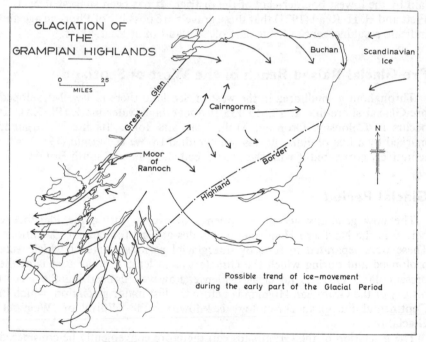

FIG. 19. *Glaciation of the Grampian Highlands*

to some extent guided by the radial systems of valleys leading outwards from the central Grampians—Loch Linnhe, Glen Orchy and Loch Awe, Glen Fyne, Loch Lomond, and the Tay, Dee and Spey valleys—but it is clear that in its upper layers at least the ice did not necessarily confine itself to movement parallel to these depressions. Striations and trains of erratics on present watersheds and even on high mountain summits, indicate that the ice could, and did, move obliquely to topographic features in response to regional pressures within the ice-sheet.

Following this epoch of maximum glaciation came the general amelioration of climate which, with some oscillations, resulted in the melting of the ice-cap and the present absence of permanent ice in Scotland. The history of this period of *Waning Glaciation*, in contrast to that of the earlier phase, is known in considerable detail and has been the subject of a vast amount of published work. As the ice-sheet diminished in extent and thickness, so the influence of topography became more pronounced, with the main ice concentrations becoming more and more confined to high ground or to districts of high precipitation. Instead of from one main ice-centre, ice next radiated from several local centres and, with further diminution, the glaciers eventually became restricted entirely to the valleys. At this stage ice-erosion over-deepened the trunk valleys which carried the main glaciers, leaving side valleys 'hanging' above them (Frontispiece) and by truncating the spurs between these side valleys produced the beautiful U-shaped profile typical of many Highland glens. Roches moutonées and striations formed during this phase of the glaciation are typically oriented parallel to the length of the glens, such striations commonly 'overprinting' those of the earlier glaciations. Conspicuous terminal and lateral moraines were formed by these valley glaciers and can readily be distinguished to this day. It is clear, however, that the transition from one great ice-sheet to valley glaciers did not take place in a uniform manner, but that there was at least one period when, after recession, Highland ice once more advanced to debouch onto the plains of the Low-lands, leaving traces of its presence in a 're-advance moraine' south of the Highland Border.

As de-glaciation continued, the valley glaciers gradually wasted until ice was confined to the high corries and, finally, disappeared, although to this day snow lies in such places late into the summer and, on the higher hills, only melts completely under exceptional conditions.

The glacial deposits accompanying the several phases of the glaciation are varied. Little remains in the central area of the Grampians of the ground-moraine of the maximum glaciation although, especially in the south-west and north-east, boulder clay on the lower ground may belong to this period. The three drift deposits of the Buchan district have already been mentioned and their preservation is probably due to the area being beyond the limits of the late valley glaciers which elsewhere swept the valleys clean of the earlier ground moraine. The presence in the lowest of the Buchan drift deposits of shelly boulder clay and also erratics of Jurassic rocks, some of which are 'rafts' of sufficient size to provide a workable source of clay, suggests that material from the Moray Firth was dredged up by the ice-sheet. In the Bay of Nigg, near Aberdeen, the lowest deposits contain crratics of Norwegian rocks, indicating that there Scandinavian ice impinged on the shores of Scotland.

During the phase of localized glacial activity which ended with the retreat of the valley glaciers, the usual morainic deposits associated with active glaciers, such as terminal and lateral moraines, were formed and successive crescentric terminal moraines commonly mark the stages of recession. It was during the period of the final dissolution of the ice, however, that the main glacial deposits of the Grampians were laid down. Vast quantities of water, released from the melting ice, poured from the glaciers and deposited spreads of fluvioglacial sands and gravels downstream from the glacier snouts. These spreads are commonly thick and have been continuously eroded from the time of their formation to the present day. Conspicuous terrace features cut in them can be seen in many of the broader Highland straths (Plate XIA).

In many cases these deposits accumulated in temporary lakes held up by

ice- or moraine-barriers and, in the Grampians, classic examples of the
former are found in the Glen Roy and Loch Tulla areas.  In the Glen Roy
example (Fig. 20, Plate XB) a glacier in Glen Spean protruded up-stream into
Glen Roy to impound a huge glacier lake in that glen and its adjacent valleys.

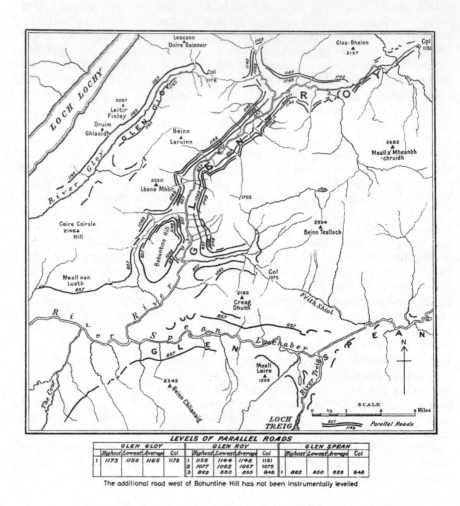

| | LEVELS OF PARALLEL ROADS | | | | | | | | | | | |
|---|---|---|---|---|---|---|---|---|---|---|---|---|
| | GLEN GLOY | | | | GLEN ROY | | | | | GLEN SPEAN | | |
| | *Highest* | *Lowest* | *Average* | Col | | *Highest* | *Lowest* | *Average* | Col | *Highest* | *Lowest* | *Average* | Col |
| 1 | 1173 | 1156 | 1165 | 1172 | 1 | 1155 | 1144 | 1148 | 1151 | | | | |
| | | | | | 2 | 1077 | 1062 | 1067 | 1075 | | | | |
| | | | | | 3 | 862 | 850 | 855 | 848 | 1 | 862 | 850 | 855 | 848 |

The additional road west of Bohuntine Hill has not been instrumentally levelled

FIG. 20.  *Map of the Parallel Roads of Glen Roy*

As the ice retreated, the level of this lake was lowered in at least three stages
by the successive disclosure of lower cols over which the water could escape.
Three well-marked 'Parallel Roads' represent strand-lines formed when the
level of the lake was controlled by one or other of the cols.

During the period of glacier melting many fine melt-water channels were
cut, some parallel to the ice margins and some cutting across spurs or valley-
divides.  These are now seen as grooves on valley sides, dry valleys or valleys
containing 'misfit' small streams.

# Raised Beaches

*Late-Glacial Beaches.* Evidence of high sea levels in part coincident with the retreat of the glaciers is widespread around the shores of North-east and West Scotland. On the south side of the Moray Firth a number of beach features are seen between 80 ft O.D. and the highest post-Glacial beaches, marking stages in the fall of the sea level from its highest point, and there are traces of possibly higher beaches up to 100 ft O.D. Near Elgin the ground appears to have been mantled by decaying ice while the sea was at the higher levels (*Sum. Prog. Geol. Surv.* for 1963). On the North Sea coast near Aberdeen the latest glacial moraines and outwash appear to have been deposited before the sea level fell to 80 ft, but it is of interest that there is evidence of a cool climate at a later stage in the form of frost structures which occur as low as 30 ft O.D. (Simpson 1948; Synge 1956). A shoreline at about 100 ft O.D. is well developed in parts of the Western Islands where great shingle beaches were formed, but the sea was excluded by ice from the upper parts of some of the firths, such as Loch Linnhe. A lower group of late-Glacial beaches between 65 ft and 45 ft is also seen on the west coast. Marine clays deposited near the ice fronts have been recorded near Aberdeen, Lossiemouth, and in the sea lochs of the west coast.

*Post-Glacial Beaches.* The withdrawal of the sea from the high levels of late-Glacial times continued until the sea-level was much lower than at present, as shown by the remains of forests, peats, and old land surfaces which are now found well below high-water mark. This episode was followed by another period of submergence which is evidenced by the well-marked post-Glacial beaches. On the west coast the maximum height of marine action is 35 ft at Loch Linnhe, decreasing gradually away from this locality. The deposits of this period contain a present-day fauna. At Balnahard at the north end of Colonsay, the sandhills contain a Neolithic floor at a height of 22 to 33 ft O.D. which may have been formed at the time of maximum post-Glacial submergence, and at Oban, where old sea-stacks occur, traces of Azilian culture have been found in raised sea caves. On the Moray coast there are beach features and old cliff lines between 15 and 25 ft O.D. together with widespread contemporaneous storm beaches.

# Recent Deposits

*Freshwater Alluvium.* Most of the streams of the Grampian Highlands are bordered by one or more terraces marking the successive levels of their flood-plains. The larger rivers, such as the Spey, Tay, Deveron, etc., flow for most of their courses through wide alluvial plains. The higher and older of these terraces are in many cases of fluvioglacial origin, as has already been described above. Deltaic deposits, except at the heads of some of the lochs, are not developed on an extensive scale.

*Peat.* Much of the higher ground is covered by a mantle of peat, which may be up to 20 ft or more in thickness, and is in many cases being subjected to denudation and wasting. In the Grampians, the lowest layer of peat contains Northern plants, the second Arctic bed of F. J. Lewis, and is followed by the main thickness of peat in which are two layers with pine-stumps which together form the Upper Forestian of Lewis. Elsewhere in Scotland, a lower forest, with birch remains, is found below the Arctic Bed.

*Blown Sand.* Where a suitable supply of raw materials was available and the nature of the sea currents and the type of climate were favourable, there have been formed deposits of blown sand. The most important of these occur on both sides of the mouth of the River Findhorn, giving the Maviston and Culbin Sandhills. The Culbin Sandhills cover an area of about six square miles and rise to a height of a hundred feet. There are dunes 10 to 30 ft high, showing conical, crescentric or ridge forms. The encroachment of the sand culminated in the great storm of the autumn of 1694, when a mansion house, sixteen farms and crofter cottages were overwhelmed. There is in this region a combination of conditions favourable for the formation of large blown-sand deposits. The Findhorn transports great quantities of sand to the sea and this material is swept on to the shelving beaches by current and tidal action. It is then caught up by the prevalent westerly winds and carried inland. In the adjacent Maviston sandhills, it is recorded that the sandhills have travelled eastwards nearly a mile during one generation. Modern stabilization techniques are being employed with success to prevent further movement of the sand.

Other large areas of blown sand are found on the Aberdeenshire coast between Fraserburgh and Peterhead, at the mouth of the River Ythan and farther south of Aberdeen. In Islay, blown sand makes an extensive spread on Big Strand, Laggan Bay.

## REFERENCES

*Pliocene:* Bremner, A. 1916; Flett, J. S. and Read, H. H. 1921; Jamieson, T. F. 1865, 1906. *See also:* 'The Geology of the Country around Banff, Huntly and Turriff' (Explanation of sheets 86 and 96) (*Mem. Geol. Survey*); High Grade Silica Rocks of the Scottish Highlands and Islands' (*Geol. Surv. Wartime Pamphlet* No. 7).
*Pre-Glacial Raised Beach:* Wright, W. B. 1911; Wright, W. B. and Peach, A. M. 1911.
*Glacial Period:* The Glacial Period in Scotland is the subject of papers and other publications too numerous to be given in a Regional Handbook. Most of these, however, are listed in one or other of the major works by J. K. Charlesworth (1955, 1957) to which the interested reader should refer for details. Raised Beaches (see below) are also dealt with by Charlesworth.
   Local detail is supplied by the Memoirs of the Geological Survey.
*Raised Beaches:* Charlesworth, J. K. 1957 (especially Chapters xlv and xlvi); Donner, J. J. 1958b, 1962; Simpson, S. 1949; Synge, F. M. 1956; *See also:* British Assoc. Adv. Sci., *The North-east of Scotland* 1963; Summary of Progress of the Geological Survey of G.B. for 1963, 1964; Memoirs of the Geological Survey.
*Recent Deposits:* Lewis, F. J. 1906, 1907, 1911. *See also:* Memoirs of the Geological Survey.

PLATE X

A. Raised Beach

B. The Parallel Roads of Glen Roy

PLATE XI

A. Fluvio-glacial deposits

B. The Ballachulish Slate Quarries

# 15. FAULTS AND EARTHQUAKES

## Faults

In the Introduction to this handbook it was pointed out that the region is confined within two major bounding fractures—the Great Glen and Highland Boundary faults respectively. As the former has been described in the companion handbook 'Scotland: The Northern Highlands' (Phemister 1960), only the latter will be dealt with here (*see* Fig. 14).

According to J. G. C. Anderson (1947), the Highland Boundary Fault proper is the most south-easterly major fault within a complex of sub-parallel major and minor fractures which, from Stonehaven to Arran, forms the south-east margin of the Scottish Highlands. To this complex he gave the name 'Highland Boundary Fracture Zone'. In places the Highland Boundary Fault is the only recognizable one present and over most of its course it effectively throws down the younger rocks of the Midland Valley, mainly Old Red Sandstone and Lower Carboniferous in age, against the older strata of the Grampian Highlands. The fault might therefore be taken to be a normal one, with downthrow to the south-east, but this is by no means the case. For instance, between Stonehaven and Loch Lomond the inclination of the fault (and of other associated faults within the fracture zone) is commonly to the north-west at steep angles and not to the south-east as would be the case for a normal fault. Over this part of its course, therefore, it is a reverse fault, or steep-angled thrust along which the rocks of the Grampians have over-ridden those of the Midland Valley. In the Loch Lomond area, however, the inclination passes through the vertical and from thence to the Clyde the hade is towards the south-east. In the same area the apparent throw of the fault is reversed when Upper Old Red Sandstone rocks on the north-west side of the fault-line near Helensburgh, together with overlying Lower Carboniferous strata, have been brought against Lower Old Red Sandstone to the south-east. These Upper Old Red Sandstone rocks, moreover, are unconformable on Dalradian Schists, while in the Midland Valley, south of the fault they overlie a great thickness of Lower Old Red Sandstone rocks. In Cowal and Bute, however, the apparent throw if the fault be normal is once more to the south-east, as Upper Old Red and Lower Carboniferous strata to the south abut against Dalradian schists to the north. George (1960) pointed out that similar anomalies of throw are found on the presumed continuation of the Highland Boundary Fault in Ireland. The fault-line is marked from place to place by a discontinuous strip of serpentinized ultra-basic rock (the Serpentine Belt) of presumed Arenig age, the strip being limited to the north-west by lesser faults of the fracture zone. Clearly, the evolution of the Highland Boundary Fault was a long and complex process.

The history of the fault has been discussed by Anderson (1947), George (1960), E. M. Anderson (1951) and Kennedy (1958). All these authors agree that there have been two main phases of movement. The earlier culminated in post-Lower, pre-Upper Old Red Sandstone times when the rocks of the former group were downfaulted against the schists and other strata of the Grampians. Then followed a period of erosion which destroyed any fault-feature which may have been present and exposed the Dalradian schists and Cambro–Ordovician strata over most of the ground immediately north-west of the fault-line. Upper Old Red Sandstone beds were then laid down, overstepping from Lower Old Red Sandstone on to Dalradian schists across the fault. In post-Lower Carboniferous times movement once more took place, in response to stresses associated with the Hercynian Orogeny, and during this phase, displacement was largely lateral, the Highland Boundary Fault acting as a sinistral-slip wrench-fault in common with several other

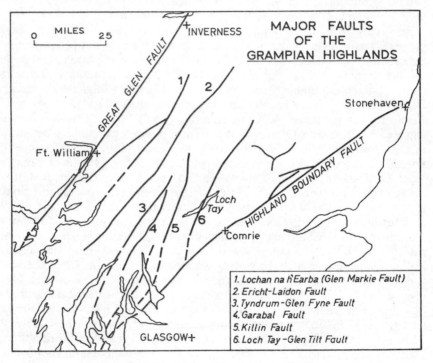

FIG. 21. *Major faults of the Grampian Highlands*

major fractures which traverse the Grampians (see below). Lateral translation of strata together with differential warping on either side of the wrench-fault is thought to account for the apparent variation in throw referred to above. J. G. C. Anderson accounted for the change in direction of hade of the fault by suggesting that the whole of the fracture zone south-westwards from Loch Lomond was tilted during the Hercynian movements.

The views of J. G. C. Anderson and T. N. George concerning the evolution of the fault differ in detail. Anderson, for instance, considered that the Highland Boundary Fracture Zone was perhaps initiated as an Arenig thrust and acted as a channel for the spilite–serpentine magma which now forms the Serpentine Belt. The movements continued thereafter with the principal displacement being, as already described, of post-Lower, pre-Upper Old Red

Sandstone age when the north-westerly (Grampian) block was thrust over a sinking block (the Midland Valley) to the south-east. A somewhat similar history is accepted by Kennedy. George, on the other hand, argued that faulting was initiated in 'post-Dalradian, pre-Arenig' times with a downthrow to the north and at this time the spilite–serpentine magma was intruded along tension-gashes. Thereafter major downthrow took place after Lower Old Red Sandstone times, the Hercynian history being much the same as that proposed by J. G. C. Anderson and E. M. Anderson.

It is difficult to reconcile the late-stage transcurrent movement postulated in these accounts with the suggestion by Friend, Harland and Hudson (1963), that in Arran to the south-west the Highland Boundary Fault is replaced by a 'monoclinal downbend of decreasing displacement'. Presumably the movement must have been replaced by folding or dissipated along other fault-lines.

*Other Faults.* The Grampian Highlands are traversed by several major north-north-east trending wrench faults of Great Glen Fault type. Notable among these are the Loch Tay–Glen Tilt, the Killin (or Bridge of Balgie), the Tyndrum–Glen Fyne, the Ericht–Laidon, and the Lochan na h'Earba (or Glen Markie) faults. In certain cases lateral (sinistral) shift of up to five miles or so can be demonstrated along these lines, but in others the presence of the fault is only indicated by broad belts of shattered rock. The main movement probably occurred in post-Lower Old Red Sandstone times and has been classed as Armorican or proto-Armorican in the grouping of E. M. Anderson (e.g. 1951). It has been shown (Smith 1961; Johnstone and Smith 1965) that the movements both pre-date and post-date the period of intrusion of dykes of Lower Old Red Sandstone age. Smith has also shown that, associated with the main faults, there is a complementary set with lesser development, trending north-north-west.

## Earthquakes

Movement along the Great Glen and Highland Boundary faults is still taking place, for they are two of the most notable lines of seismic activity in Britain (Davison 1924; Dollar 1950). Strong earthquakes occurred in the Inverness district in 1816, 1888, 1890, 1901 and 1934 while numerous shocks have been recorded in the neighbourhood of Comrie on the Highland Boundary Fault.

### REFERENCES

Anderson, E. M. 1951; Anderson, J. G. C. 1947; Davison, C. 1924; Dollar, A. T. J. 1950; Friend, P. F., Harland, W. B. and Hudson, J. P. 1963; George, T. N. 1960; Kennedy, W. Q. 1958; Smith, D. I. 1961; Johnstone, G. S. and Smith, D. I. 1965.

G*

# 16. ECONOMIC MINERALS

The Grampian Highlands are not rich in minerals of high intrinsic value and such minerals as are at present worked are mainly those which, although of low value per ton, are available in bulk—limestone, sand and gravel, brick clay and roadstone. The ferrous and non-ferrous ore bodies so far known have all been investigated in fairly recent years by possible users but despite modern prospecting techniques none has been found to be of sufficient interest to warrant exploitation under present economic conditions. Demand and methods of beneficiation change, however, and it would be unwise to dismiss the occurrences as of no potential value. They have therefore been included in the following list.

*Barytes.* Barytes is not common in the Grampian Highlands. It occurs in places in the crush-rock of late faults, and a lenticular vein has been recorded from Balfreish, in the Nairn valley, in the limestone at the base of the Middle Old Red Sandstone.

*Bauxitic Clay.* Bauxitic clay occurs in the Carboniferous rocks of the Machrihanish area (*see* Ch. 11).

*Brick Clay.* Superficial deposits have been and are still being worked for brick clay in widespread areas of coastal Aberdeenshire, Banffshire and Morayshire. Sources include boulder clay, fluvioglacial deposits, raised beach deposits and alluvium. The nature of the deposits makes assessment of reserves difficult but it was considered in 1946 that such reserves were 'probably ample'. Quality is variable, again a feature of the type of deposit, but on average is probably somewhat poor although suitable for tiles and drainage pipes, etc., and bricks of moderate strength. (*Geol. Surv. Wartime Pamphlet,* No. 47).

*Building Stone.* Good quality freestone is still worked and even exported from quarries in the Permian sandstone near Hopeman, Elgin. Rather poorer quality material has been extensively worked in the Elgin area from sandstones of Middle and Upper Old Red Sandstone and Triassic ages. In Aberdeenshire the Caledonian granites are the best and most highly exploited building stones: workings are focused on Aberdeen itself and have given rise to an associated stone-polishing industry. Many of the Highland metamorphic and intrusive rocks have been locally used as building materials, but, with the notable exception of the aforementioned granites, their use is generally limited by an over abundance of parting planes or by intractability. (*Mem. Geol. Surv., Min. Resources,* vol. xxxii).

*Chromite and Magnesite.* Chrome iron ore, disseminated through antigorite–serpentine, was once worked on the farm of Corrycharmaig, four miles north-west of Killin. This small mass of serpentine includes local areas in which magnesium carbonate (magnesite or breunnerite) occurs in considerable quantities. While the locality is not likely to be of interest as a source of chrome ore, it has been suggested that natural association of chromite, antigorite and magnesite may provide raw material for the manufacture of chrome–magnesia refractory bricks. Local abundance of chromite is also recorded from the serpentine body at Green Hill between Glen Nochty and Kindie in Aberdeenshire. The deposit is probably not of importance as an ore of chromium, but as at Corrycharmaig, the rock may be of interest as a raw material for chrome refractories. (*Geol. Surv. Wartime Pamphlet*, No. 9, and Supplement).

*Coal.* There is a small coalfield of Carboniferous age at Machrihanish, Argyllshire (*see* Ch. 11).

*Copper.* In Islay at Kilsleven Mine, copper ore was worked in the eighteenth century and intermittently since then. Around Loch Fyne several copper veins have been worked; near Kilmartin several veins up to 4 ft thick cut an epidiorite mass and consist of quartz and calcite carrying chalcopyrite. Another old mine near Inverary, originally opened for copper, provided between 1854 and 1867 a fair quantity of nickeliferous pyrrhotite; similar copper–nickel ore occurs at Craignure south-west of Inveraray. On the east side of Loch Fyne around Kilfinan the Loch Tay Limestone and associated schists are in places impregnated with copper ores, malachite and sulphides, which have been worked. Other trials for copper ore have been made near Lochgilphead and Ardrishaig.

At Tomnadashan on the south side of Loch Tay the late Marquis of Breadalbane worked a deposit of chalcopyrite, etc. associated with a granitic rock and a lamprophyre which cut the schists. Recent investigations, however, did not result in much hope for the economic exploitation of the material. Copper ores are also found in association with some of the lead and zinc occurrences of the Grampians (see below). (*Mem. Geol. Surv. Min. Resources*, vol. xvii).

*Diatomite.* Small deposits of diatomite are widespread but the only major potential source is the Muir of Dinnet, between Ballater and Aboyne in Aberdeenshire, where the diatomite was recognized in 1880 and has been worked spasmodically on a small scale since then. Thicknesses of deposit range from 1 to 15 feet but are generally 2 to 3 ft; peat overburden may be as much as 15 ft. Quality would not seem to be up to the highest standards. Reserves may exist elsewhere at sites formerly occupied by lochs, but these could only be discovered and assessed by boring. (*Geol. Surv. Wartime Pamphlet*, No. 5).

*Dolomite.* (*see* Limestone).

*Feldspar.* A pegmatite vein near Portsoy in Banffshire was formerly worked as a source of alkali feldspar and reserves are not exhausted. Other pegmatites of possible value occur in the Central Grampians near Loch Laggan and Dalwhinnie. (*Geol. Surv. Wartime Pamphlet*, No. 44).

*Fluorspar.* Although fluorite is widely distributed as a component of veins in Banffshire and Aberdeenshire, frequently in calcareous rocks, and as a matrix of the New Red Sandstones of the Elgin district (*see* Chapter 12), it seems that there are only two sources of economic potential: (a) the disused Abergairn mine (see also Lead) near Ballater, Aberdeenshire, where dumps of gangue material are composed largely of fluorite and (b) the Permian sandstone of Greenbrae Quarry and district, near Hopeman, Morayshire; parts of this sandstone have a matrix consisting entirely of fluorite which may make up as much as 36 per cent by weight of the rock.

*Garnet.* Vast quantities of rock containing garnet occur in the Grampian

Highlands but none of the material so far examined has proved of interest as an abrasive.

*Iron and Manganese Ore.* Various attempts have been made over a period of more than two centuries to work the Lecht Mines near Tomintoul for either iron or manganese. The three-mile long vein appears to be never more than a few feet in width and to be essentially vertical. The iron occurs as hematite and limonite, the manganese as psilomelane and wad. Local concentrations of up to 52 per cent iron and 12½ per cent manganese have been recorded but the vein tends to be siliceous and rich in phosphorus. Veins of similar composition occur at Ardnilly on the River Spey, 2 miles north of Craigellachie. Trial pits were dug in about 1870 but no further action was taken. At the Mull of Oa, Islay, a network of manganite veins traversing quartzite was worked at one time. Siliceous magnetite or hematite ironstone occurs in assocation with pillow lavas of the Cambro–Ordovician rocks of the Highland Border, while at Dalroy in the Nairn valley a deposit of manganese ore of variable thickness fills hollows in the schist floor below the Old Red Sandstone. Lesser deposits of iron or manganese ore are known from other localities in the Grampians. (*Mem. Geol. Surv., Min. Resources,* vol. xi).

*Kyanite.* Kyanite, and the kindred minerals andalusite and sillimanite, are used in the manufacture of some kinds of refractory materials. It is possible that certain occurrences of these minerals in the Grampians might prove of economic interest, although considerable beneficiation of the bulk material would certainly be needed.

*Lead and Zinc.* In Islay, veins containing galena, blende, pyrites and chalcopyrite were worked until 1862. They occur in the Islay Limestone and Esknish Slates. On both sides of Loch Fyne in Argyllshire, veins with galena and blende, together with copper ores, have been worked at many localities; the ore deposits are usually associated with the Ardrishaig Phyllites and adjacent quartzite and occur in two types, true veins and metasomatic replacements. Other old lead mines are situated in Glenorchy and Glen Creran. The most celebrated lead deposits of the Central Highlands are those of Tyndrum in Perthshire, where several parallel veins traverse the schists, and are closely associated with one of the faults of the Tyndrum Fault zone (*see* p. 87). The veins have a maximum thickness of 20 ft, and have a gangue of quartz, calcite and barytes; the primary ores are galena, zinc–blende chalcopyrite and pyrites, the two former occurring in some cases as ribs 2 ft wide. Despite efforts to re-open the mines in the present century and several attempts to assess their potential by modern prospecting methods, the workings are at present abandoned. Small trials have been opened on many thin lead–zinc veins in Perthshire. In Aberdeenshire argentiferous galena and zinc–blende in a vein of calcite and fluorspar were at one time worked at Abergairn, Deeside. A quartz-vein, 12 ft across, with galena and iron–pyrites has been noted in the Dulnan valley, Strathspey. Near Lossiemouth galena occurs disseminated through the Cherty Rock and the adjacent Triassic sandstones and was at one time worked. Many Scottish lead–zinc veins carry silver (2 to 10 oz to the ton). Traces of gold are also found locally. A complex lead–zinc–copper ore, formerly worked at Stronchullin, near Ardrishaig, Argyllshire, showed the exceptional assay value of 4 oz of gold to the ton, but the rich pocket soon became exhausted. (*Mem. Geol. Surv., Min. Resources,* vol. xvii; Barnet, G. W. T. 1959).

*Limestone and Dolomite*. Limestones of the Dalradian Assemblage are quarried in several parts of the Grampian Highlands; notably in the counties of Inverness (Ballachulish Limestone), Argyllshire (Ballachulish Limestone, Loch Tay Limestone, Shira Limestone, Islay Limestone), Perthshire (Blair Atholl Limestone) and Banffshire (Boyne, and other limestones). The output is mainly used as ground agricultural lime and road chips. Reserves are considerable although the existing quarries probably exploit the best sites to meet present demand.

Dolomite was formerly worked in Appin (Appin Dolomite) but working ceased because of variation in quality. Dolomite is also found in the Blair Atholl Limestone of Perthshire. (*Mem. Geol. Surv., Min. Resources*, vol. xxv).

*Magnesite*. See 'Chromite and Magnesite', above.

*Manganese*. See 'Iron and Manganese Ore', above.

*Peat*. Deposits of peat are both widespread and abundant throughout the area, especially the 'Hill peat' type on the higher uplands although there are also considerable areas of 'Basin peat' on the plateau districts of Aberdeenshire.

Utilization as fuel, generally by individual users, has not been important in the present century but persists in some areas and has a specialized application in the distillation of whisky. Commercial production for fuel and also for peat litter and horticultural usage has been undertaken in northern Aberdeenshire but this kind of exploitation is generally hampered by the inaccessibility of large-scale deposits and the costs of transportation. (*Geol. Surv. Wartime Pamphlet*, No. 36).

*Precious Metals and Gemstones*. Both native gold and argentiferous galena occur in association with some of the copper–lead–zinc (q.v.) sulphide mineralization of Perthshire. It is doubtful if any deposit is worthy of economic exploitation.

Upper Deeside in Aberdeenshire is the type locality for the variety of quartz known as Cairngorm. A once profitable industry has declined in the face of competition from cheap imported stones and the apparent exhaustion of source veins in many of the best localities. Beryls are not infrequent in the same area. The host rock for both gemstones is Caledonian 'Newer Granite'.

Garnets are widely distributed in the Dalradian schists but they are not of gemstone quality.

*Road Metal*. Road metal is obtained from quarries in the less schistose varieties of metamorphic rock; granulites, quartzites, grits, epidiorites, limestones, etc., or in the igneous rocks: Newer Granites, Lower Old Red Sandstone minor intrusions, or dykes of Permo–Carboniferous or of Tertiary age. It is probably true to say that adequate quality roadstone is obtainable everywhere within a moderate distance of the demand throughout the Grampians (Phemister and others 1946).

*Sands and Gravels*. A wide range of source materials is included under the term Sand and Gravel. Deposits are invariably superficial and include morainic material, fluvioglacial, fluviatile and marine alluvium and aeolian sand. The age of deposits ranges from Pleistocene to Recent, together with gravels of probable Pliocene age occurring near Turriff, Fyvie and Peterhead. There are vast reserves in the north-eastern parts of the Grampians and in the Spean Bridge–Loch Laggan area (Plate XIA), although quality varies and suitable material for the specification in demand may have to be sought.

The south-western parts of the area are less well endowed although material

from the extensive raised beaches might well meet some of the local require-
ments. (*Geol. Surv. Wartime Pamphlet*, No. 30; Anderson 1943).

*Serpentine.* Serpentine intrusions occur in association with the Dalradian
succession in Banffshire, Aberdeenshire, Angus and Perthshire, and in the
Cambro–Ordovician Serpentine Belt along the Highland Border. Besides its
traditional use as an ornamental stone, for which it was worked, notably at
Portsoy, this rock has an economic potentiality as a source material for
refractory brick manufacture. Much of the Highland Border material is
carbonated or otherwise impure.

*Silica Rock.* The purer Highland quartzites would probably be serviceable
for silica-brick making, although trials with material from Islay have not
proved successful. The Appin Quartzite near Kentallen was formerly
quarried for use in grinding-tubs in the pottery industry. Quartz veins occur
in many parts of the Grampian Highlands, but are generally thin and imper-
sistent. A thick vein of high purity occurs near Dalwhinnie, but is rather
inaccessible. A siliceous sandstone of considerable purity, belonging to the
Limestone Coal Group, occurs in the Machrihanish Coalfield, and has been
mined, mainly as a source of moulding sand. (*Geol. Surv. Wartime Pamphlet*,
No. 7).

*Slate.* Reserves of slate are abundant in the north-eastern and south-
western Grampians (Plate XIB) and along the Highland Border, although
workings have been generally discontinued as a result of competition from
first the Welsh product, with its more refined quality, and later from manu-
factured roofing materials. (*Geol. Surv. Wartime Pamphlet*, No. 40).

*Talc*, with its varieties steatite (massive, fine-grained talc), soapstone or
potstone (impure talcose rock), is normally found as an alteration
product of serpentine and the two usually occur together in the field. The
most important workings have been in crush zones of the Portsoy serpentine
but small quantities have been recorded from numerous serpentine bodies in
Aberdeenshire, Angus, and Perthshire. Of these, the serpentine extending
from Banff to Cortachy on the Highland Boundary carries abundant talc on
shear planes, whilst part of a small intrusion at Corrycharmaig, near Killin
has been altered to an aggregate of talc and breunnerite from which the talc
could be freed by crushing and froth floatation. Recent investigations at the
latter locality suggest that the reserves of talc are too small to be of commercial interest. (*Geol. Surv. Wartime Pamphlet*, No. 9).

## REFERENCES

Geological Survey publications: *Memoirs of the Geological Survey* covering the Grampian
Highlands area and the papers there cited; *Special Reports on the Mineral Resources of
Great Britain*, vols. i, iv, xi, xvii, xxxii, xxxiii, xxxv, xxxvii; *Wartime Pamphlets of the
Geological Survey*, Nos. 5, 6, 7, 9, 13, 30, 36, 40, 44, 47.
    For full titles of the above see 'General Bibliography'.
    Many of these publications are out of print, but photostatic abstracts may be had from:
                          The Assistant Director,
                          Geological Survey of Great Britain,
                          19 Grange Terrace,
                          Edinburgh, 9.
*See also:*
    Anderson, J. G. C. 1943; Barnet, G. W. T. 1959; Dunham, K. C. 1954; Harris, G. F.
1888; Howe, J. A. 1910; Phemister, J., Guppy, Eileen M. and Marwick, A. H. D. 1946;
Robertson, R. H. S. and Whitehead, T. H. 1954; Robertson, T. 1945; Russell, A. 1936;
Scottish Council (Development and Industry) 1961.

# 17. GENERAL BIBLIOGRAPHY

ALEXANDER, H. 1950. *Scottish Mountaineering Club Guide—The Cairngorms.* 3rd Edit. Edinburgh.

ALLAN, D. A. 1928. The Geology of the Highland Border from Tayside to Noranside. *Trans. Roy. Soc. Edin.,* 56, 57.

—— 1940. The Geology of the Highland Border from Glen Almond to Glen Artney. *Trans. Roy. Soc. Edin.,* 60, 171.

ALLISON, A. 1933. The Dalradian Succession in Islay and Jura. *Quart. J. Geol. Soc.,* 89, 125.

—— 1936. The Tertiary Dykes of the Craignish Area, Argyll. *Geol. Mag.,* 73, 73.

—— 1940. Loch Awe Succession and Tectonics: Kilmartin–Tayvallich–Danna. *Quart. J. Geol. Soc.,* 96, 423.

ANDERSON, E. M. 1923. The Geology of the Schists of the Schichallion District. *Quart. J. Geol. Soc.,* 79, 423.

—— 1951. *The Dynamics of Faulting and Dyke Formation, with Applications in Britain.* 2nd Edit. Edinburgh.

—— 1952. Lineation and its relation to sub-crustal Convection Currents. *Geol. Mag.,* 89, 113.

ANDERSON, J. G. C. 1935a. The Dalradian Succession in the Pass of Brander District, Argyll. *Geol. Mag.,* 72, 74.

—— 1935b. The Marginal Intrusions of Ben Nevis, etc. *Trans. Geol. Soc. Glas.,* 19, 225.

—— 1935c. The Arrochar Intrusive Complex. *Geol. Mag.,* 72, 263.

—— 1937a. The Etive Granite Complex. *Quart. J. Geol. Soc.,* 93, 487.

—— 1937b. Intrusions of the Glen Falloch Area. *Geol. Mag.,* 74, 458.

—— 1942. The Stratigraphical Order of the Dalradian Schists near the Highland Border. *Trans. Geol. Soc. Glas.,* 20, 223.

—— 1943. *Scottish Sands and Gravels,* Tintagel.

—— 1945a. The Dalradian Rocks of Arran. *Trans. Geol. Soc. Glas.,* 20, 264.

—— 1945b. High grade Silica Rocks of the Scottish Highlands and Islands. *Wartime Pamphlet* No. 7. *Geol. Surv.*

—— 1947. The Geology of the Highland Border, Stonehaven to Arran. *Trans. Roy. Soc. Edin.,* 61, 497.

—— 1948. Stratigraphical Nomenclature of Scottish Metamorphic Rocks. *Geol. Mag.,* 85, 89.

—— 1949. The Gareloch Readvance Moraine. *Geol. Mag.,* 86, 239.

—— 1953. The Stratigraphical Succession and Correlation of the Late pre-Cambrian and Cambrian of Scotland and Ireland. *Les Subdivisions et les Corrélations de l'Antécambrien. Rep. 19th Intern. Geol. Congr.* (Algiers) 1952, Sect. 1, fasc. 1.

—— 1956. The Moinian and Dalradian rocks between Glen Roy and Monadhliath Mountains, Inverness-shire. *Trans. Roy. Soc. Edin.,* 63, 15.

—— and PRINGLE, J. 1944. The Arenig Rocks of Arran, and their Relationship to the Dalradian Series. *Geol. Mag.,* 81, 81.

—— and TYRRELL, G. W. 1937. Xenolithic Minor Intrusions in the Loch Lomond District. *Trans. Geol. Soc. Glas.,* 19, 373.

ATHERTON, M. P. 1964. The garnet isograd in pelitic rocks and its relationship to metamorphic facies. *Am. Miner.,* 49, 1331.

BAILEY, E. B. 1910. Recumbent Folds in the Schists of the Scottish Highlands. *Quart. J. Geol. Soc.,* 66, 586.

—— 1913. The Loch Awe Syncline (Argyllshire). *Quart. J. Geol. Soc.,* 69, 280.

—— 1914. The Ballachulish Fold near the Head of Loch Creran (Argyllshire). *Quart. J. Geol. Soc.,* 70, 321.

—— 1917. The Islay Anticline (Inner Hebrides). *Quart. J. Geol. Soc.,* 72 for 1916, 132.

—— 1922. The Structure of the South-west Highlands of Scotland. *Quart. J. Geol. Soc.,* 78, 82.

—— 1923. The Metamorphism of the South-west Highlands. *Geol. Mag.,* 60, 317.

—— 1925. Perthshire Tectonics: Loch Tummel, Blair Atholl and Glen Shee. *Trans. Roy. Soc. Edin.,* 53, 671.

—— 1928. Schist Geology: Braemar, Glen Clunie and Glen Shee. *Trans. Roy. Soc. Edin.,* 55, 737.

BAILEY. E. B., 1930. New Light on Sedimentation and Tectonics. *Geol. Mag.*, **67**, 77.
—— 1934a. The Interpretation of Scottish Scenery. *Scot. Geogr. Mag.*, **50**, 308.
—— 1934b. West Highlands Tectonics: Loch Leven to Glen Roy. *Quart. J. Geol. Soc.*, **90**, 462.
—— 1936. The Ballachulish Lag at Callert, Loch Leven. *Geol. Mag.*, **73**, 412.
—— 1938. Eddies in Mountain Structure. *Quart. J. Geol. Soc.*, **94**, 607.
—— 1958. Some chemical aspects of south-west Highland Devonian igneous rocks. *Bull. Geol. Surv. Gt. Brit.*, No. 15, 1.
—— 1960. The Geology of Ben Nevis and Glen Coe. 2nd Edit. *Mem. Geol. Surv.*
—— and HOLTEDAHL, O. 1938. *Regionale Geologie der Erde, Bd., 2; Palaeozoische Tafeln und Gebirge. Abt. ii, North-western Europe Caledonides:* Leipzig.
—— and McCALLIEN, W. J. 1934. The Metamorphic Rocks of North-east Antrim. *Trans. Roy. Soc. Edin.*, **58**, 163.
—— 1937. Perthshire Tectonics: Schiehallion to Glen Lyon. *Trans. Roy. Soc. Edin.*, **59** 79.
—— and MACGREGOR, M. 1912. The Glen Orchy Anticline (Argyllshire). *Quart. J. Geol. Soc.*, **68**, 164.
—— and MAUFE, H. B. 1916. The Geology of Ben Nevis and Glen Coe. *Mem. Geol. Surv.*
BAIRD, P. D. and LEWIS, W. V. 1957. The Cairngorm floods, 1956, summer solifluction and distributary formation. *Scot. Geogr. Mag.*, **73**, 91.
BARNETT, G. W. T. 1959. Lead in Islay *in Future of non-ferrous mining in Gt. Britain and Ireland.* London. (Inst. Min. and Met.).
BARROW, G. 1892. On Certain Gneisses with Round-grained Oligoclase and their Relation to Pegmatite. *Geol. Mag.*, N.S. Dec. 3, **9**, 64.
—— 1893. On an Intrusion of Muscovite-biotite Gneiss in the South-eastern Highlands of Scotland and its accompanying Metamorphism. *Quart. J. Geol. Soc.*, **49**, 330.
—— 1901. On the Occurrence of Silurian (?) Rocks in Forfarshire and Kincardineshire along the Eastern Border of the Highlands. *Quart. J. Geol. Soc.*, **57**, 328.
—— 1904. Moine Gneisses of the East Central Highlands and their position in the Highland Sequence. *Quart. J. Geol. Soc.*, **50**, 400.
—— 1912. On the Geology of Lower Deeside and the Southern Highland Border. *Proc. Geol. Assoc.*, **23**, 274.
BEMMELEN, R. W. VAN. 1937. The Cause and Mechanism of Igneous Intrusion: with some Scottish Examples. *Trans. Geol. Soc. Glas.*, **19**, 479.
BLACK, G. P. and MACKENZIE, D. H. 1957. Supposed Unconformities in the Old Red Sandstone of Western Moray. *Geol. Mag.*, **94**, 170.
BLUNDELL, D. J. and READ, H. H. 1958. Palaeomagnetism of the younger gabbros of Aberdeenshire and its bearing on their deformation. *Proc. Geol. Assoc.*, **69**, 191.
BOULENGER, G. A. 1903. Some Reptilian Remains from the Trias of Elgin. *Phil. Trans. Roy. Soc.*, **196**, 175.
BOWES, D. R. 1962. Kentallenite–lamprophyre–granite age relations at Kentallen, Argyll. *Geol. Mag.*, **99**, 119.
—— and JONES, K. A. 1958. Sedimentary features and tectonics in the Dalradian of western Perthshire. *Trans. Edin. Geol. Soc.*, **17**, 133.
——, KINLOCH, E. D. and WRIGHT, A. E. 1964. Rhythmic amphibole overgrowths in appinites associated with explosion-breccias in Argyll. *Mineralog. Mag.*, **33**, 963.
—— MACDONALD, A. D., MATHESON, G. D. and WRIGHT, A. E. 1963. An explosion-breccia–appinite complex at Gleann Charnan, Argyll. *Trans. Geol. Soc. Glas.*, **25**, 19.
—— and WRIGHT, A. E. 1961. An explosion-breccia complex at Back Settlement near Kentallen, Argyll. *Trans. Edin. Geol. Soc.*, **18**, 293.
—— and WRIGHT, A. E. 1962. Washout structures in the Dalradian near Kentallen, Argyll. *Geol. Mag.*, **99**, 53.
BREMNER A. 1912. The Physical Geology of the Dee Valley. *Aberdeen Nat. Hist. Antiquar. Soc.*, No. 1.
—— 1915. Capture of the Geldie by the Feshie. *Scot. Geogr. Mag.*, **31**, 589.
—— 1916. Problems in the Glacial Geology of North-east Scotland. *Trans. Edin. Geol. Soc.*, **10**, 344.
—— 1919. A Geographical Study of the High Plateau of the South-eastern Highlands. *Scot. Geogr. Mag.*, **35**, 331.
—— 1921. The Physical Geology of the Don Basin. *Aberdeen Nat. Hist. Antiquar. Soc.*, No. 2.
—— 1928. Further Problems in the Glacial Geology of North-eastern Scotland. *Trans. Edin. Geol. Soc.*, **12**, 147.
—— 1934a. The Glaciation of the Abernethy Forest. *Trans. Edin. Geol. Soc.*, **13**, 1.
—— 1934b. The Glaciation of Moray and Ice Movements in the North of Scotland. *Trans. Edin. Geol. Soc.*, **13**, 17.
—— 1939a. The Late-Glacial Geology of the Tay Basin from Pass of Birnam to Grandtully and Pitlochry. *Trans. Edin. Geol. Soc.*, **13**, 473.

BREMNER, A. 1939b. Notes on the Glacial Geology of East Aberdeenshire. *Trans. Edin. Geol. Soc.*, **13**, 474.
—— 1942. The Origin of the Scottish River System. *Scot. Geogr. Mag.*, **58**, pt. i, 15–19, pt. ii, 54–59, pt. iii, 99–103.
BROWN, P. E. and others. 1965. Potassium-argon age patterns of the British Caledonides. *Proc. Yorks. Geol. Soc.*, **35**, 103.
BRITISH ASSOC. ADV. SCI. 1963. *The North-east of Scotland*. Aberdeen.
BUCHAN, S. 1932. On Some Dykes in East Aberdeenshire. *Trans. Edin. Geol. Soc.*, **12**, 323.
CADELL, H. M. 1886. The Dumbartonshire Highlands. *Scot. Geogr. Mag.*, **2**, 337.
—— 1913. *The Story of the Forth*. Edinburgh.
CAMERON, J. 1945. Structural Features of the Grey Granites of Aberdeenshire. *Geol. Mag.*, **82**, 189.
CAMPBELL, R. 1911. Preliminary Note on the Geology of South-eastern Kincardineshire. *Geol. Mag.*, **8**, 63.
—— 1913. The Geology of South-eastern Kincardineshire. *Trans. Roy. Soc. Edin.*, **48**, 923.
CHARLESWORTH, J. K. 1955. The Late-glacial History of the Highlands and Islands of Scotland. *Trans. Roy. Soc. Edin.*, **42**, 769.
—— 1957. *The Quaternary Era*. London.
CHINNER, G. A. 1960. Pelitic gneisses with varying ferrous/ferric ratios from Glen Clova, Angus, Scotland. *J. Petrology*, **1**, 178.
—— 1961. The origin of sillimanite in Glen Clova, Angus. *J. Petrology*, **2**, 312.
—— 1962. Almandine in thermal aureoles. *J. Petrology*, **3**, 316.
CLOUGH, C. T., MAUFE, H. B. and BAILEY, E. B. 1909. The Cauldron-Subsidence of Glen Coe and the associated Igneous Phenomena. *Quart. J. Geol. Soc.*, **65**, 611.
CROFT, W. N. and GEORGE, E. A. 1959. Blue-Green Algae from the Middle Devonian of Rhynie, Aberdeenshire. *Bull. Brit. Mus. (Nat. Hist.). Geol.*, **3**, 339.
CUMMINS, W. A. and SHACKLETON, R. M. 1955. The Ben Lui Recumbent Syncline (S.W. Highlands). *Geol. Mag.*, **92**, 353.
CUNNINGHAM-CRAIG, E. H. 1904. Metamorphism in the Loch Lomond District. *Quart. J. Geol. Soc.*, **60**, 10.
DAKYNS, J. R. and TEALL, J. J. H. 1892. On the Plutonic Rocks of Garabal Hill and Meall Breac. *Quart. J. Geol. Soc.*, **48**, 104.
DAVISON, C. 1924. *A History of British Earthquakes*. Cambridge.
DEER, W. A. 1938a. The Composition and Paragenesis of the Hornblendes of the Glen Tilt Complex, Perthshire. *Mineralog. Mag.*, **25**, 56.
—— 1938b. The Diorites and associated Rocks of the Glen Tilt Complex, Perthshire. *Geol. Mag.*, **75**, 174.
—— 1950. The Diorites and associated Rocks of the Glen Tilt Complex, Perthshire. II. Diorites and Appinites. *Geol. Mag.*, **87**, 181.
—— 1953. The Diorites and associated Rocks of the Glen Tilt Complex, Perthshire: III. Hornblende-schist and Hornblendite Xenoliths in the Granite and Diorite. *Geol. Mag.*, **90**, 27.
DEWEY, J. F. 1961. A note concerning the age of the Dalradian metamorphism of western Ireland. *Geol. Mag.*, **98**, 399.
——, and PHILLIPS, W. E. A. 1963. A Tectonic Profile across the Caledonides of South Mayo. *Liv. & Manch. Geol. J.*, **3**, 237.
DIXON, J. S. 1905. *Final Report of the Royal Commission on Coal Supplies*. H.M. Stationery Office, London. 6.
DOLLAR, A. T. J. 1950. Catalogue of Scottish Earthquakes, 1916–1949. *Trans. Geol. Soc. Glas.*, **21**, 283.
DONNER, J. J. 1958a. Loch Mahaick, a late glacial site in Perthshire. *New Phytologist*, **57**, 183.
—— 1958b. The geology and vegetation of late-Glacial retreat stages in Scotland. *Trans. Roy. Soc. Edin.*, **63**, 221.
—— 1962. On the post-glacial history of the Grampian highlands of Scotland. *Soc. Sci. Fennica, Comm. Biol.*, **24**, 29.
DUNHAM, K. C. 1954. Age-relations of the Epigenetic Mineral Deposits of Britain. *Trans. Geol. Soc. Glas.*, **21**, 395.
DURNO, S. E. 1962. Pollen analysis of peat deposits in the eastern Grampians. *Scot. Geogr. Mag.*, **75**, 102.
ELLES, GERTRUDE L. 1926. The Geological Structure of Ben Lawers and Meall Corranaich (Perthshire). *Quart. J. Geol. Soc.*, **82**, 304.
—— 1935. The Loch na Cille Boulder Bed and its place in the Highland Succession. *Quart. J. Geol. Soc.*, **91**, 111.
—— and TILLEY, C. E. 1930. Metamorphism in Relation to Structure in the Scottish Highlands. *Trans. Roy. Soc. Edin.*, **56**, 621.
EVANS, J. W. and STUBBLEFIELD, C. J. (Edit.) 1929. *Handbook of the Geology of Great Britain*. London.

# 96 The Grampian Highlands

FARQUHAR, O. C. 1953. From Dolerite to Diorite: Older Granite Activity near Ellon, Aberdeenshire. *Geol. Mag.*, **90**, 393.

FITZPATRICK, E. A. 1965. An Interglacial soil at Tiendland, Morayshire. *Nature*, **207**, No. 4997, 621.

FLETT, J. S. and READ, H. H. 1921. Tertiary Gravels of the Buchan District of Aberdeenshire. *Geol. Mag.*, **58**, 215.

FRANCIS, G. H. 1956. Facies Boundaries in Pelite at the Middle Grades of Regional Metamorphism. *Geol. Mag.*, **93**, 353–68.

FRIEND, P. F., HARLAND, W. B. and HUDSON, J. P. 1963. The Old Red Sandstone and the Highland Boundary in Arran, Scotland. *Trans. Edin. Geol. Soc.*, **19**, 363.

GEIKIE, A. 1879. On the Old Red Sandstone of Western Europe. *Trans. Roy. Soc. Edin.*, **28**, 345.

—— 1891. Anniversary Address of the President. *Quart. J. Geol. Soc.*, **47**, 72.

—— 1892. *Explanatory Notes to Accompany a new Geological Map of Scotland*. Edinburgh.

—— 1901. *The Scenery of Scotland viewed in connection with its Physical Geology*. London.

GEIKIE, J. 1894. *The Great Ice Age*. 3rd Edit. London.

GEOLOGICAL SURVEY MEMOIRS ETC.
*One-inch Sheet Memoirs.* The full title in each case is 'The Geology of . . .' (Explanation of Sheet . . .):
Islay etc. (19 and 27, with the western part of 20), 1907; Knapdale, Jura and North Kintyre (28, with parts of 27 and 29), 1911; Colonsay and Oronsay etc. (35, with part of 27), 1911; The Seaboard of Mid-Argyll (36), 1909; Mid-Argyll (37), 1905; Oban and Dalmally (45), 1908; Ben Nevis and Glen Coe (53) 2nd Edit., 1960; Corrour and the Moor of Rannoch (54), 1923; Blair Atholl, Pitlochry and Aberfeldy (55), 1905; Upper Strathspey, etc. (64), 1913; Braemar, Ballater and Glen Clova (65), 1912; Mid-Strathspey and Strathdearn (74), 1915; West Aberdeenshire, Banffshire, etc. (75), 1896; Central Aberdeenshire (76), 1890; Lower Findhorn and Lower Strath Nairn (84 and part of 94), 1923; Lower Strathspey (85), 1902; Banff, Huntly and Turriff (86 and 96), 1923; North-east Aberdeenshire (87), 1886; Northern Aberdeenshire (97), 1882.
*District Memoirs.*
The Geology of Cowal, 1897 (deals with parts of sheets 29 and 37); The Pre-Tertiary Geology of Mull, Loch Aline and Oban, 1925 (includes sheet 44).
*Special Reports on the Mineral Resources of Great Britain.*
Vol. i: Tungsten and Manganese Ores, 3rd Edit. 1923.
Vol. iv: Fluorspar, 4th Edit. 1952.
Vol. xi: The Iron Ores of Scotland, 1920.
Vol. xvii: The Lead, Zinc, Copper and Nickel Ores of Scotland, 1921.
Vol. xxxii: The Granites of Scotland, 1939.
Vol. xxxiii: Synopsis of the Mineral Resources of Scotland, 1940.
Vol. xxxv: The Limestones of Scotland, 1949.
Vol. xxxvii: The Limestones of Scotland: Chemistry and Petrography, 1956.
*Wartime Pamphlets of the Geological Survey.*
No. 5: Diatomite, 1940.
No. 6: Dolomite and Brucite-Marble in the Scottish Highlands, 1940.
No. 7: High-Grade Silica Rocks of the Scottish Highlands and Islands, 2nd Edit., 1945.
No. 9: Talc, Other Magnesian Minerals and Chromite, associated with British Serpentines, 2nd Edit., 1941; re-issue, revised, 1946.
No. 13: Limestones of Scotland:
 Area IV, South-west Highlands and Islands, 2nd Edit., 1945.
 Area V, Central Grampians, 1944.
 Area VI, Banffshire and North-east Grampians, 1944.
No. 30: Sands and Gravels of Scotland:
 Quarter-inch Sheet 9: Stonehaven–Perth–Dundee, 1945.
 Quarter-inch Sheet 12: Elgin–Banff–Aberdeen, 1943.
No. 36: Peat Deposits of Scotland: Part I, General Account, 1943.
No. 40: Scottish Slates, 1944.
No. 44: Scottish Sources of Alkali Feldspar, 1945.
No. 47: Brick Clays of North-east Scotland, 1946.
*see also*
*The Summary of Progress of the Geological Survey of Great Britain* for the years cited in the text.

GEORGE, T. N. 1955. Drainage in the Southern Uplands: Clyde, Nith, Annan. *Trans. Geol. Soc. Glas.*, **22**, 1.

—— 1960. The Stratigraphical Evolution of the Midland Valley. *Trans. Geol. Soc. Glas.*, **24**, 32.

GEORGE, T. N. 1963. Palaeozoic Growth of the British Caledonides. *The British Caledonides*. London and Edinburgh.

GIBB, A. W. 1909. On the Relation of the Don to the Avon at Inchrory, Banffshire. *Trans. Edin. Geol. Soc.*, **9**, 227.

GILETTE, B. J., LAMBERT, R. ST. J. and MOORBATH, S. 1961. A geochronological study of the metamorphic complexes of the Scottish Highlands. *Quart. J. Geol. Soc.*, **117**, 233.

GLENTWORTH, R. 1954. The soils of the country round Banff, Huntly and Turriff (Lower Banffshire and north-west Aberdeenshire). *Mem. Soil Surv. Scot.*

GREEN, J. F. N. 1924. The Structure of the Bowmore-Portaskaig District of Islay. *Quart. J. Geol. Soc.*, **80**, 72.

—— 1931. The South-west Highland Sequence. *Quart. J. Geol. Soc.*, **87**, 513.

GREGORY, J. W. 1910. Work for Glasgow Geologists—The Problems of the South-western Highlands. *Trans. Geol. Soc. Glas.*, **14**, 1.

—— 1913. *The Nature and Origin of Fiords*. London.

—— 1928. The Geology of Loch Lomond. *Trans. Geol. Soc. Glas.*, **18**, 301.

—— 1930. The Sequence in Islay and Jura. *Trans. Geol. Soc. Glas.*, **18**, 420.

—— 1931. *Dalradian Geology*. London.

GUNN, W., CLOUGH, C. T. and HILL, J. B. 1897. The Geology of Cowal. *Mem. Geol. Surv.*

HACKMAN, B. D. and KNILL, J. L. 1962. Calcareous algae from the Dalradian of Islay. *Palaeontology*, **5**, 262.

HARDIE, W. G. 1952. The Lochaber Series south of Loch Leven, Argyllshire. *Geol. Mag.*, **89**, 273.

—— 1955. The Problem of Facies Changes and Sliding, south of Loch Leven, Argyllshire. *Geol. Mag.*, **92**, 506.

—— 1963. Explosion-Breccias near Stob Mhic Mhartuin, Glen Coe, Argyll and their bearing on the origin of the nearby flinty crush rock. *Trans. Edin. Geol. Soc.*, **19**, 426.

HARKER, A. 1918. Presidential Address. *Quart. J. Geol. Soc.*, **73**, 86.

—— 1929. *In* EVANS, J. W. and STUBBLEFIELD, C. J. *Handbook of the Geology of Great Britain*. London.

—— 1932. *Metamorphism*. London. (2nd Edit., 1939).

HARRIS, A. L. 1962. Dalradian geology of the Highland border near Callander. *Bull. Geol Surv. Gt. Brit.*, No. 19, 1.

—— 1963. Structural Investigations in the Dalradian rocks between Pitlochry and Blair Atholl. *Trans. Edin. Geol. Soc.*, **19**, 256.

—— and RAST, N. 1960. The evolution of quartz fabrics in the metamorphic rocks of Central Perthshire. *Trans. Edin. Geol. Soc.*, **18**, 51.

HARRIS, G. F. 1888. *Granite and our Granite Industries*. London.

HARRY, W. T. 1952. An unusual Appinitic Sill near Killin, Perthshire. *Geol. Mag.*, **89**, 41.

—— 1957. A Re-examination of Barrow's Older Granites in Glen Clova, Angus. *Trans. Roy. Soc. Edin.*, **63**, 393.

—— 1965. The form of the Cairngorm Granite Pluton. *Scot. J. Geol.*, **1**, 1.

HATCH, F. H. and WELLS, A. K. 1926. *The Petrology of the Igneous Rocks*. London.

HENDERSON, S. M. K. 1938. The Dalradian Succession of the Southern Highlands. *Rep. Brit. Assoc.* (Cambridge 1938), 424.

HILL, J. B. and KYNASTON H. 1900. Kentallenite and its Relations to other Igneous Rocks in Argyllshire. *Quart. J. Geol. Soc.* **56**, 531.

HINXMAN L. W. 1901. The River Spey. *Scot. Geogr. Mag.* **17**, 185.

HOLGATE N. 1951. The Glen Banvie Igneous Complex of Perthshire. *Quart. J. Geol. Soc.*, **106**, 433.

HOLTEDAHL O. 1952. The Structural History of Norway and its relation to Great Britian. *Quart. J. Geol. Soc.*, **108**, 65.

HORNE, J. 1894. The Character of the High Level Shell-bearing Deposits at Clava. *Rep. Brit. Assoc.* for 1893, 483.

—— 1901. Recent Advances in Scottish Geology. *Rep. Brit. Assoc.* for 1901, 615.

HOWE, J. A. 1910. *Geology of Building Stones*. London.

HOWIE, R. A. 1964. Some orthopyroxenes from Scottish metamorphic rocks. *Mineralog. Mag.*, **33**, 903.

HUENE, F. VON. 1908. On the Age of the Reptile Faunas contained in the Magnesian Conglomerate at Bristol and in the Elgin Sandstones. *Geol. Mag.*, **5**, 99.

—— 1910a. Uber einen echten Rhynchocephalen aus der Trias von Elgin. *Neues Jahrb. f. Mineralogie*, **2**, 29.

—— 1910b. Ein primitiver Dinosaur aus der mittleren Trias von Elgin. *Geol. Palaeont. Abh.*, **8**, 23.

HUTCHISON, A. G. 1933. The Metamorphism of the Deeside Limestone, Aberdeenshire. *Trans. Roy. Soc. Edin.*, **57**, 557.

HUTTON, C. O. 1938. On the nature of Withamite from Glen Coe, Scotland. *Mineralog. Mag.*, **25**, 119.

HUXLEY, T. H. 1859–1887. Descriptions of the Elgin Reptiles. *Quart. J. Geol. Soc.*, **15,** 1859; **23,** 1867; **25,** 1869; **31,** 1875; **43,** 1887.
—— 1877. The Crocodilian Remains found in the Elgin Sandstones, etc. *Monograph Geol. Survey,* No. iii.
JAMIESON, T. F. 1858. On the Pleistocene Deposits of Aberdeenshire. *Quart. J. Geol. Soc.,* **14,** 509.
—— 1860. On the Drift and Rolled Gravel of the North of Scotland. *Quart. J. Geol. Soc.,* **16,** 347.
—— 1865. On the History of the Last Geological Changes in Scotland. *Quart. J. Geol. Soc.,* **21,** 164.
—— 1874. On the Last stages of the Glacial Period in North Britain. *Quart. J. Geol. Soc.,* **30,** 317.
—— 1906. The Glacial Period in Aberdeenshire and the Southern Border of the Moray Firth. *Quart. J. Geol. Soc.,* **62,** 13.
JEHU, T. J. and CAMPBELL, R. 1917. The Highland Border Rocks of the Aberfoyle District. *Trans. Roy. Soc. Edin.,* **52,** 175.
JOHNSON, M. R. W. 1962. Relations of movement and metamorphism in the Dalradians of Banffshire. *Trans. Edin. Geol. Soc.,* **19,** 29.
—— 1963. Some time relations of movement and metamorphism in the Scottish Highlands. *Geol. en Mijn.,* **42,** 121.
—— and HARRIS, A. L. 1965. Is the Tay Nappe post Arenig? *Scot. J. Geol.,* **1,** 217.
—— and STEWART, F. H. 1960. On Dalradian structures in north-east Scotland. *Trans. Edin. Geol. Soc.,* **18,** 94.
—— (Editors). 1963. *The British Caledonides.* London and Edinburgh.
JOHNSTONE, G. S. 1955. A Re-investigation of the Steall Area, Upper Glen Nevis. *Trans. Edin. Geol. Soc.,* **16,** 167.
—— and WRIGHT, J. E. 1955. A Section through the Iltay Boundary Slide in the Errochty Hydro-Electric Tunnel. *Bull. Geol. Surv. Gt. Brit.,* No. 7, 101.
—— 1957. The geology of the tunnels of the Loch Sloy hydro-electric scheme. *Bull. Geol. Surv. Gt. Brit.,* No. 12, 1.
—— and SMITH, D. I. 1965. Geological Observations concerning the Breadalbane Hydro-Electric Project, Perthshire. *Bull. Geol. Surv. Gt. Brit.,* No. 22, 1.
JONES, K. A. 1961. Origin of albite porphyroblasts in the rocks of the Ben More-Am Binnein area, western Perthshire, Scotland. *Geol. Mag.,* **98,** 41.
—— 1964. Metamorphism in the Ben More-Am Binnein area, western Perthshire, Scotland. *Quart. J. Geol. Soc.,* **120,** 51.
JUDD, J. W. 1873. The Secondary Rocks of Scotland. *Quart. J. Geol. Soc.,* **29,** 97.
KENNEDY, W. Q. 1946. The Great Glen Fault. *Quart. J. Geol. Soc.,* **102,** 41.
—— 1948. The significance of thermal structure in the Scottish Highlands. *Geol. Mag.,* **85,** 229.
—— 1958. The Tectonic Evolution of the Midland Valley of Scotland. *Trans. Geol. Soc. Glas.,* **23,** 107.
KIDSTON, R. 1923. On the Vascular Plants of the Chert Band of Rhynie. *Trans. Edin. Geol. Soc.,* **11,** 257.
—— and LANG, W. H. 1917. On Old Red Sandstone Plants showing Structure from the Rhynie Chert Bed, Aberdeenshire. *Trans. Roy. Soc. Edin.,* **51,** 761; 1920, **52,** 603; 1921, **53,** 831.
—— 1924. Notes on Fossil Plants from the Old Red Sandstone of Scotland: III. On two Species of *Pachytheca. Trans. Roy. Soc. Edin.,* **53,** 608.
KING, B. C. and RAST, N. 1956. Tectonic styles in the Dalradians and Moines of parts of the central Highlands of Scotland. *Proc. Geol. Assoc.,* **66,** 243.
—— 1956. The small-scale structures of south-eastern Cowal, Argyllshire. *Geol. Mag.,* **93,** 185.
KNILL, J. L. 1959a. Axial and marginal sedimentation in geosynclinal basins. *J. Sediment. Petrology,* **29,** 317.
—— 1959b. The tectonic pattern in the Dalradian of the Craignish–Kilmelfort district, Argyllshire. *Proc. Geol. Soc. Lond.,* No. 1569, 83.
—— 1960a. Palaeocurrents and sedimentary facies of the Dalradian meta-sediments of the Craignish–Kilmelfort district. *Proc. Geol. Assoc.,* **70,** 273.
—— 1960b. A classification of cleavages with special references to the Craignish district of the Scottish Highlands. *Rep. 21st Internat. Geol. Congr.,* (Copenhagen), **18,** 317.
—— 1960c. The tectonic pattern in the Dalradian of the Craignish–Kilmelfort district, Argyllshire. *Quart. J. Geol. Soc.,* **115,** 339.
—— 1961. Joint drags in mid-Argyllshire. *Proc. Geol. Assoc.,* **72,** 13.
—— and KNILL, D. C. 1958. Some discordant fold structures from the Dalradian of Craignish, Argyll, and Rosguill, Co. Donegal. *Geol. Mag.,* **95,** 497.
KVALE, A. 1953. Linear Structures and their relation to Movement in the Caledonides of Scandinavia and Scotland. *Quart. J. Geol. Soc.,* **109,** 51.

LACAILLE, A. D. 1950. The Chronology of the Deglaciation of Scotland. *Proc. Geol. Assoc.*, **61**, 121.
LANG, W. H. 1922. The Flora of the Rhynie Chert Bed. *Rep. Brit. Assoc.* for 1921, 419.
LEE, G. W. and PRINGLE, J. 1932. A Synopsis of the Mesozoic Rocks of Scotland. *Trans. Geol. Soc. Glas.*, **19**, 158.
LEWIS, F. J. 1906–11. The Plant Remains in the Scottish Peat Mosses. *Trans. Roy. Soc. Edin.*, **45**, 335; **46**, 33; **47**, 793.
LINTON, D. L. 1951. Problems of Scottish Scenery. *Scot. Geogr. Mag.*, **67**, 65.
  *(This paper has a comprehensive Bibliography.)*
——— 1959. Morphological contrasts of eastern and western Scotland. In *Geographical Essays in memory of Alan G. Ogilvie*, 16. London–Edinburgh.
——— 1959. Measures of corrie (cirque) development in Scotland. *Bull. Geol. Soc. Amer.*, **70**, 1808.
McCALLIEN, W. J. 1928. Preliminary Account of the Post-Dalradian Geology of Kintyre. *Trans. Geol. Soc. Glas.*, **28**, 40.
——— 1929. The Metamorphic Rocks of Kintyre. *Trans. Roy. Soc. Edin.*, **56**, 409.
——— 1931. A Contribution to the Correlation of the Dalradian Rocks of Scotland and Ireland. *Geol. Mag.*, **68**, 126.
——— 1932. The Kainozoic Igneous Rocks of Kintyre. *Geol. Mag.*, **69**, 49.
——— 1935. The Metamorphic Rocks of Inishowen, Co. Donegal. *Proc. Roy. Irish Acad.*, **42**, 437.
——— 1937. The Geology of the Rathmullan District, Co. Donegal. *Proc. Roy. Irish Acad.*, **44**, 56.
——— and ANDERSON, R. B. 1930. The Carboniferous Sediments of Kintyre. *Trans. Roy. Soc. Edin.*, **56**, 599.
MACGREGOR, A. G. 1929. Metamorphism around the Lochnagar Granite, Aberdeenshire. *Rep. Brit. Assoc.* for 1928, 553.
——— 1931. Clouded Feldspars and Thermal Metamorphism. *Mineralog. Mag.*, **22**, 524.
——— 1937. The Carboniferous and Permian Volcanoes of Scotland. *Bull. Volcanol.*, **1**, 50.
——— 1960. Divisions of the Carboniferous on Geological Survey Scottish maps. *Bull. Geol. Surv. Gt. Brit.*, No. 16, 127.
——— and KENNEDY, W. Q. 1932. The Morven–Strontian Granite. *Sum. Prog. Geol. Surv. Gt. Brit.* for 1931, pt. 2, 105.
MACGREGOR, S. M. A. and ROBERTS, J. 1963. Dalradian Pillow Lavas, Ardwell Bridge, Banffshire. *Geol. Mag.*, **100**, 17.
McINTYRE, D. B. 1951. The Tectonics of the Area between Grantown and Tomintoul (Mid-Strathspey). *Quart. J. Geol. Soc.*, **107**, 1.
MACKENZIE, D. H. 1957. On the relationship between migmatization and structure in mid-Strathspey. *Geol. Mag.*, **94**, 177.
MACKIE, W. 1897. The Sands and Sandstones of Eastern Moray. *Trans. Edin. Geol. Soc.*, **7**, 148.
——— 1901. The Pebble Band of the Elgin Trias and its wind-worn pebbles. *Rep. Brit. Assoc. Glasgow*, 650.
——— 1908. Evidence of Contemporaneous Volcanic Action in the Banffshire Schists. *Trans. Edin. Geol. Soc.*, **9**, 93.
——— 1914. The Rock Series of Craigbeg and Ord Hill, Rhynie, Aberdeenshire. *Trans. Edin. Geol. Soc.*, **10**, 205.
——— 1923. The Principles that Regulate the Distribution of Particles of Heavy Minerals, etc. *Trans. Edin. Geol. Soc.*, **11**, 138.
MACKINDER, H. J. 1907. *Britain and the British Seas.* 2nd Edit. Oxford.
McLACHLAN, G. R. 1951. The Aegerine-granulites of Glen Lui, Braemar, Aberdeenshire. *Mineralog. Mag.*, **29**, 476.
MACNAIR, P. 1908. *The Geology and Scenery of the Grampians.* Glasgow.
MANSON, W. and CALVER, M. A. 1957. On the occurrence of a marine band in the *Anthraconaia modiolaris* Zone of the Scottish Coal Measures. *Bull. Geol. Surv. Gt. Brit.*, No. 12, 66.
MAUFE, H. B. 1910. The Geological Structure of Ben Nevis. *Sum. Prog. Geol. Surv. Gt. Brit.* for 1909, 80.
MERCY, E. L. P. 1963. The Geochemistry of some Caledonian Granitic and Metasedimentary Rocks. *In The British Caledonides.* London and Edinburgh.
MILLER, J. A. 1961. Age of metamorphism of Moine schists. *Geol. Mag.*, **98**, 85.
MOULD, DAPHNE D. C. P. 1946. The Geology of the Foyers "Granite" and the Surrounding Country. *Geol. Mag.*, **83**, 249.
MUNRO, H. T. and OTHERS. 1953. *Scottish Mountaineering Club Guide—Munro's Tables of the 3,000 ft mountains of Scotland and Other Tables of Lesser Heights.* Edinburgh.
MYKURA, W. 1965. The age of the lower part of the New Red Sandstone of South-West Scotland. *Scot. J. Geol.*, **1**, 9.

NEWTON, E. T. 1893. On some New Reptiles from the Elgin Sandstones. *Phil. Trans. Roy. Soc.*, **184**, 431.

——— 1894. Reptiles of the Elgin Sandstone, Description of two new Genera. *Phil. Trans. Roy. Soc.*, **185**, 573.

NICOL, J. 1852. On the Geology of the Southern Portion of the Peninsula of Cantyre Argyllshire. *Quart. J. Geol. Soc.*, **8**, 406.

NOCKOLDS, S. R. 1934. The Contaminated Tonalites of Loch Awe, Argyll. *Quart. J. Geol. Soc.*, **90**, 302.

——— 1941. The Garabal Hill–Glen Fyne Igneous Complex. *Quart. J. Geol. Soc.*, **96**, 451.

——— 1946. The Order of Crystallization of the Minerals in some Caledonian Plutonic and Hypabyssal Rocks. *Geol. Mag.*, **83**, 206.

——— and MITCHELL, R. L. 1948. The Geochemistry of some Caledonian Plutonic Rocks. *Trans. Roy. Soc. Edin.*, **61**, 533.

OGILVIE, A. G. 1914. Physical Geography of the Entrance to Inverness Firth. *Scot. Geogr. Mag.*, **30**, 21.

PANTIN, H. M. 1956. The Petrology of the Ben Vrackie Epidiorites and their Contact Rocks. *Trans. Geol. Soc. Glas.*, **22**, 48.

——— 1957. A variety of quartzite from Craig-choinnich Lodge, near Blair Atholl, Perthshire. *Geol. Mag.*, **94**, 409.

——— 1961. The stratigraphy and structure of the Blair Atholl–Ben a' Gloe area, Perthshire, Scotland. *Trans. Roy. Soc. New Zealand*, **88**, 597.

PEACH, B. N. and HORNE, J. 1910. The Scottish Lakes in Relation to the Geological Features of the Country, *in Bathymetrical Survey of the Scottish Fresh-Water Lochs*, Sir J. Murray and L. Pullar, Edinburgh, **1**, 457.

——— and HORNE, J. 1930. *Chapters on the Geology of Scotland*. Oxford.

PHEMISTER, J. 1960. The Northern Highlands. 3rd Edit. *British Regional Geology, Geol. Surv.*

———, GUPPY, EILEEN M. and MARKWICK, A. H. D. 1946. Roadstone: Geological Aspects and Physical Tests. *Road Research: Special Report* No. 3 (D.S.I.R.).

PHEMISTER, T. C., FRASER, W. E. and WILLIAMSON, D. H. 1960. Dalradian Metamorphism and Structure—Stonehaven to Aberdeen. *Rep. 21st Internat. Geol. Congr.* (Copenhagen), **13**, 352.

PHILLIPS, F. C. 1930. Some Mineralogical and Chemical changes Induced by Progressive Metamorphism in the Green Bed Group of the Scottish Dalradian. *Mineralog. Mag.*, **22**, 239.

——— 1956. Structural petrology and problems of the Caledonides. *Adv. Sci.*, **12**, 571.

PRINGLE, J. 1940. The Discovery of Cambrian Trilobites in the Highland Border Rocks near Callander, Perthshire. *Adv. Sci.*, **1**, 252.

——— 1942. The Relationship of the Green Conglomerate to the Margie Grits in the North Esk, near Edzell; and on the probable Age of the Margie Limestone. *Trans. Geol. Soc. Glas.*, **20**, 136.

——— 1944. The Carboniferous Rocks of Glas Eilean, Sound of Islay, Argyllshire: with an Appendix on the Petrography by E. B. Bailey. *Trans. Geol. Soc. Glas.*, **20**, 249.

——— 1952. On the Occurrence of Permian Rocks in Islay and North Kintyre. *Trans. Edin. Geol. Soc.*, **14**, 297.

——— and MACGREGOR, M. 1940. The Outlier of Carboniferous Rocks at Bridge of Awe, Argyllshire. *Trans. Geol. Soc. Glas.*, **20**, 72.

RAMSAY, D. M. 1962. Microfabric studies from the Dalradian Rocks of Glen Lyon, Perthshire. *Trans. Edin. Geol. Soc.*, **19**, 166.

——— 1964. Deformation of Pebbles in the Lower Old Red Sandstone Conglomerates adjacent to the Highland Boundary Fault. *Geol. Mag.*, **101**, 228.

RAST, N. 1958a. Metamorphic history of the Schichallion Complex (Perthshire). *Trans. Roy. Soc. Edin.*, **63**, 413.

——— 1958b. The tectonics of the Schichallion complex. *Quart. J. Geol. Soc.*, **114**, 25.

——— and PLATT, J. I. 1957. Cross-folds. *Geol. Mag.*, **94**, 159.

READ, H. H. 1923. The Petrology of the Arnage District in Aberdeenshire. *Quart. J. Geol. Soc.*, **79**, 446.

——— 1924. On Certain Xenoliths associated with the Contaminated Rocks of the Huntly Mass, Aberdeenshire. *Geol. Mag.*, **61**, 433.

——— 1927. The Igneous and Metamorphic History of Cromar, Deeside, Aberdeenshire. *Trans. Roy. Soc. Edin.*, **55**, 317.

——— 1928. The Highland Schists of Middle Deeside and East Glen Muick. *Trans. Roy. Soc. Edin.*, **55**, 755.

——— 1931. On Corundum-Spinel Xenoliths in the Gabbro of Haddo House, Aberdeenshire. *Geol. Mag.*, **68**, 446.

——— 1935. The Gabbros and Associated Xenolithic Complexes of the Haddo House District, Aberdeenshire. *Quart. J. Geol. Soc.*, **91**, 591.

READ, H. H. 1936. The Stratigraphical Order of the Dalradian Rocks of the Banffshire Coast. *Geol. Mag.*, **72**, 468.
—— 1940. Metamorphism and Igneous Action. *Adv. Sci.*, London, **1**, 223.
—— 1951. Mylonitisation and Cataclasis in Acidic Dykes in the Insch (Aberdeenshire) Gabbro and its Aureole. *Proc. Geol. Assoc.*, **62**, 237.
—— 1952. Metamorphism and Migmatisation in the Ythan Valley, Aberdeenshire. *Trans. Edin. Geol. Soc.*, **15**, 265.
—— 1955. The Banff Nappe. *Proc. Geol. Assoc.*, **66**, 1.
—— 1957. The dislocated south-western margin of the Insch igneous mass, Aberdeenshire. *Proc. Geol. Assoc.*, **67**, 73.
—— 1961. Aspects of Caledonian Magmatism in Britain. *Liv. & Manch. Geol. J.*, **2**, 653.
——, BREMNER, A., CAMPBELL, R. and GIBB, A. W. 1923. Records of the Occurrence of Boulders of Norwegian Rocks in Aberdeenshire and Banffshire. *Trans. Edin. Geol. Soc.*, **11**, 230.
—— and FARQUHAR, O. C. 1952. The Geology of the Arnage District (Aberdeenshire): a reinterpretation. *Quart. J. Geol. Soc.*, **107**, 423.
—— —— 1956. The Buchan anticline of the Banff nappe of Dalradian rocks in north-east Scotland. *Quart. J. Geol. Soc.*, **112**, 131.
—— and HAQ, B. T. 1963. The distribution of Trace-Elements in the Dunite-Syenite Differentiated Series of the Insch Complex, Aberdeenshire. *Proc. Geol. Assoc.*, **74**, 203.
—— —— 1965. Notes, Mainly Geochemical, on the Granite–Diorite Complex of the Insch Igneous Mass, with an Addendum on the Aberdeenshire Quartz-Dolerites. *Proc. Geol. Assoc.*, **76**, 13.
—— and MACGREGOR, A. G. 1948. The Grampian Highlands. 2nd Edit. *British Regional Geology, Geol. Surv.*
——, SADASHIVAIAH, M.S. and HAQ, B. T. 1962. Differentiation in the olivine-gabbro of the Insch Mass, Aberdeenshire. *Proc. Geol. Assoc.*, **72**, 391.
—— —— 1965. The Hypersthene-Gabbro of the Insch Complex, Aberdeenshire. *Proc. Geol. Assoc.*, **76**, 1.
REYNOLDS, DORIS L. 1936. Demonstrations in Petrogenesis from Kiloran Bay, Colonsay: I. The Transfusion of Quartzite. *Mineralog. Mag.*, **24**, 367.
—— 1942. The Albite-Schists of Antrim and their Petrogenetic Relationship to Caledonian Orogenesis. *Proc. Roy. Irish Acad.*, **48**, 43.
RICHARDSON, J. B. 1962. Spores with bifurcate processes from the Middle Old Red Sandstone of Scotland. *Palaeontology*, **5**, 171.
—— 1965. Middle Old Red Sandstone spore assemblages from the Orcadian basin, north-east Scotland. *Palaeontology*, **7**, 559.
RICHEY, J. E. 1939. The Dykes of Scotland. *Trans. Edin. Geol. Soc.*, **13**, 402.
ROBERTS, J. L., and TREAGUS, J. E. 1964. A Re-Interpretation of the Ben Lui Fold. *Geol. Mag.*, **101**, 512
ROBERTSON, R. H. S. and WHITEHEAD, T. H. 1954. Report of the Mineral Resources Panel on serpentine and olivine-rock in Scotland. *Scottish Council (Devel. and Ind.)*. Edinburgh, 1954.
ROBERTSON, T. 1945. Scottish Mineral Deposits, *in Hydro-Electric Industries for Scotland* (Scottish Local Section of Institute of Metals, Glasgow).
RUSSELL, A. 1936. Notes on the Occurrence of Fluorite in Aberdeenshire and Banffshire. *Mineralog. Mag.*, **24**, 307.
SABINE, P. A. and WATSON, JANET, 1965. Isotopic age-determinations of rocks from the British Isles, 1955–64. *Quart. J. Geol. Soc.*, **121**, 477.
SADASHIVAIAH, M. S. 1950. Olivine-bearing and other basic Hornfelses around the Insch Igneous Mass, Aberdeenshire. *Geol. Mag.*, **87**, 121.
—— 1954a. The Form of the Eastern End of the Insch Igneous Mass, Aberdeenshire. *Geol. Mag.*, **91**, 137.
—— 1954b. The Granite–Diorite Complex of the Insch Igneous Mass, Aberdeenshire. *Geol. Mag.*, **91**, 286.
SCOTTISH COALFIELDS COMMITTEE. 1944. *Scottish Coalfields*. Scottish Home Department. Edinburgh.
SCOTTISH COUNCIL (DEVELOPMENT AND INDUSTRY). 1961. *Natural Resources in Scotland*. (A Symposium—Chairman L. A. Elgood.)
SHACKLETON, R. M. 1948. Overturned Rhythmic Banding in the Huntly Gabbro of Aberdeenshire. *Geol. Mag.*, **85**, 358.
—— 1958. Downward facing structures of the Highland Border. *Quart. J. Geol. Soc.*, **113**, 361.
SIMPSON, J. B. 1953. *Sum. Prog. Geol. Surv. Gt. Brit.* for 1951, 42.
SIMPSON, S. 1949. The Glacial Deposits of Tullos and the Bay of Nigg, Aberdeen. *Trans. Roy. Soc. Edin.*, **61**, 687.
—— 1955. A Re-interpretation of the Drifts of North-East Scotland. *Trans. Edin. Geol. Soc.*, **16**, 189.

SIMPSON, S. and TOWNSHEND, G. K. 1952. The Tunnelling Stream and the Melt-water Channels at Muchalls, Kincardineshire. *Trans. Edin. Geol. Soc.*, **14**, 396.

SITTER, L. U. DE. 1956. *Structural Geology*. London.

SMITH, A. J. and RAST, N. 1958. Sedimentary dykes in the Dalradian of Scotland. *Geol. Mag.*, **95**, 234.

SMITH, D. I. 1961. Patterns of minor faults in the south Central Highlands of Scotland. *Bull. Geol. Surv. Gt. Brit.*, No. 17, 145.

SNELLING, N. J. 1957. A note on the composition of staurolite from the Caenlochan schists. *Mineralog. Mag.*, **31**, 603.

STEWART, A. D. 1962a. On the Torridonian sediments of Colonsay and their relationships to the main outcrop in North-west Scotland. *Liv. & Manch. Geol. J.*, **3**, 121.

—— 1962b. Greywacke Sedimentation in the Torridonian of Colonsay and Oronsay. *Geol. Mag.*, **99**, 399.

STEWART, F. H. 1947. The Gabbroic Complex of Belhelvie in Aberdeenshire. *Quart. J. Geol. Soc.*, **102**, 465.

—— and JOHNSON, M. R. W. 1960. The structural problem of the younger gabbros of north-east Scotland. *Trans. Edin. Geol. Soc.*, **18**, 104.

STONE, M. 1957. The Aberfoyle Anticline, Callander, Perthshire. *Geol. Mag.*, **94**, 265.

STUBBLEFIELD, C. J. 1958. Problèmes des séries intermédiaires en Grande-Bretagne. In *Les Relations entre Précambrien et Cambrien*. Paris C.N.R.S.

STURT, B. A. 1961. The geological structure of the area south of Loch Tummel. *Quart. J. Geol. Soc.*, **117**, 131.

—— 1962. The composition of garnets from pelitic schists in relation to the grade of regional metamorphism. *J. Petrology*, **3**, 181.

—— and HARRIS, A. L. 1961. The metamorphic history of the Loch Tummel area, central Perthshire. *Liv. & Manch. Geol. J.*, **2**, 689.

SUESS, E. 1904. *The Face of the Earth*. Oxford.

SUESS, F. E. 1931. A Suggested Interpretation of Scottish Caledonide Structure. *Geol. Mag.*, **68**, 71.

SUTTON, J. 1960. Some structural problems in the Scottish Highlands. *Rep. 21st Internat. Geol. Congr.* (Copenhagen), **18**, 371.

—— 1963. Some events in the Evolution of the Caledonides. *In The British Caledonides*. London and Edinburgh.

—— and WATSON, JANET. 1955. The deposition of the Upper Dalradian rocks of the Banffshire coast. *Proc. Geol. Assoc.*, **66**, 101.

—— 1956. The Boyndie Syncline of the Dalradian of the Banffshire coast. *Quart. J. Geol. Soc.*, **112**, 103.

SYNGE, F. M. 1956. The glaciation of north-east Scotland. *Scot. Geogr. Mag.*, **72**, 129.

TARLO, L. B. 1961. Psammosteids from the Middle and Upper Devonian of Scotland. *Quart. J. Geol. Soc.*, **117**, 193.

TASCH, P. 1957. Flora and fauna of the Rhynie Chert; a paleoecological re-evaluation of published evidence. *Univ. Stud. munic. Univ. Wichita* No. 36.

TAYLOR, W. 1920. A New Locality for Triassic Reptiles, etc. *Trans. Edin. Geol. Soc.*, **11**, 11.

THOMSON, J. 1865. On the Geology of the Campbeltown District. *Trans. Geol. Soc. Glas.*, **11**, 76.

TILLEY, C. E. 1924. Contact-Metamorphism in the Comrie Area of the Perthshire Highlands. *Quart. J. Geol. Soc.*, **80**, 22.

—— 1925. A preliminary survey of Metamorphic Zones in the Southern Highlands of Scotland. *Quart. J. Geol. Soc.*, **81**, 100.

TOIT, A. L. DU. 1905. The Lower Old Red Sandstone Rocks of the Balmaha–Aberfoyle Region. *Trans. Edin. Geol. Soc.*, **8**, 323.

TRAQUAIR, R. H. 1896. The Extinct Vertebrate Animals of the Moray Firth Area *in* J. A. Harvie-Brown and T. E. Buckley's *Vertebrate Fauna of the Moray Basin*. **2**, Edinburgh.

—— 1897. Additional Notes on the Fossil Fishes of the Upper Old Red Sandstone of the Moray Firth Area. *Proc. Roy. Phys. Soc. Edin.*, **13**, 376.

TREAGUS, J. E. 1964. Notes on the Structure of the Ben Lawers Synform. *Geol. Mag.*, **101**, 260.

TRUEMAN, A. E. 1954. *Coalfields of Great Britain*. London.

URRY, W. D. and HOLMES, A. 1941. Age Determination of Carboniferous Basic Rocks of Shropshire and Colonsay. *Geol. Mag.*, **78**, 45.

VOGT, T. 1930. On the Chronological Order of Deposition of the Highland Schists. *Geol. Mag.*, **67**, 68.

VOLL, G. 1960. New work on petrofabrics. *Liv. & Manch. Geol. J.*, **2**, 503.

—— 1964. Deckenbau und fazies im Schottischen Dalradian. *Geol. Rdsch.*, **2**, 590.

WALKER, A. D. 1961. Triassic Reptiles from the Elgin Area: *Stagonolepis, Dasygnathus* and their allies. *Phil. Trans. Roy. Soc.*, (B) **244**, 103.

WALKER, A. D., 1964. Triassic Reptiles from the Elgin Area: *Ornithosuchus* and the origin of Carnosaurs. *Phil. Trans. Roy. Soc.*, (B) **248**, 53.
WALKER, F. 1935. The Late Palaeozoic Quartz-dolerites and Tholeiites of Scotland. *Mineralog. Mag.*, **24**, 131.
—— 1939. The Geology of Maiden Island, Oban. *Trans. Edin. Geol. Soc.*, **13**, 475.
—— 1961. The Islay–Jura Dyke Swarm. *Trans. Geol. Soc. Glas.*, **24**, 121.
—— and DAVIDSON, C. F. 1935. Marginal and Contact Phenomena of the Dorback Granite. *Geol. Mag.*, **72**, 49.
—— and PATTERSON, E. M. 1959. A differentiated boss of alkali dolerite from Cnoc Rhaonastil, Islay. *Mineralog. Mag.*, **32**, 140.
WATSON, D. M. S. 1908. *Coccosteus minor*, Hugh Miller, in the Old Red Sandstone of Dalcross, Inverness-shire. *Geol. Mag.*, **5**, 431.
—— 1909. The Trias of Moray. *Geol. Mag.*, **6**, 102.
—— and HICKLING, G. 1914. On the Triassic and Permian Rocks of Moray. *Geol. Mag.*, **2**, 399.
WATSON, J. 1911. *British and Foreign Building Stones*. Cambridge.
WATSON, JANET. 1963. Some problems concerning the Evolution of the Caledonides of the Scottish Highlands. *Proc. Geol. Assoc.*, **74**, 213.
—— 1964. Conditions in the Metamorphic Caledonides during the Period of Late-orogenic cooling. *Geol. Mag.*, **101**, 457.
WATT, W. R. 1914. The Geology of the Country around Huntly, Aberdeenshire. *Quart. J. Geol. Soc.*, **70**, 266.
WEISS, L. E. and McINTYRE, D. B. 1957. Structural geometry of Dalradian rocks at Loch Leven, Scottish Highlands. *J. Geol.*, **65**, 575.
WESTOLL, T. S. 1937. On a specimen of *Eusthenopteron* from the Old Red Sandstone of Scotland. *Geol. Mag.*, **74**, 507.
—— 1940. New Scottish Material of *Eusthenopteron*. *Geol. Mag.*, **77**, 65.
—— 1948. Vertebrate Palaeontology: *Guide to Excursion C.16. Internat. Geol. Congr. XVIII (Gt. Britain)*.
—— 1951. The Vertebrate Bearing Strata of Scotland. *Rept. XVIIIth Internat. Geol. Cong.*, *(Gt. Britain)*, 1948, pt. 11.
—— 1964. The Old Red Sandstone of North-eastern Scotland. *Adv. Sci.*, **20**, 446.
WHITTLE, G. 1936. The Eastern End of the Insch Igneous Mass, Aberdeenshire. *Proc. Liv. Geol. Soc.*, **17**, 64.
WHITTEN, E. H. T. 1959. A study of two directions of folding; the structural geology of the Monadhlaith and mid-Strathspey. *J. Geol.*, **67**, 14.
WILLIAMSON, D. H. 1953. Petrology of Chloritoid and Staurolite rocks north of Stonehaven, Kincardineshire. *Geol. Mag.*, **90**, 353.
WILLIAMSON, W. O. 1935. The Composite Gneiss and contaminated Granodiorite of Glen Shee, Perthshire. *Quart. J. Geol. Soc.*, **91**, 382.
—— 1936. Some Minor Intrusions of Glen Shee, Perthshire. *Geol. Mag.*, **73**, 145.
WISEMAN, J. D. H. 1934. The Central and South-west Highland Epidiorites, etc. *Quart. J. Geol. Soc.*, **90**, 354.
WOOD, D. S. 1964. Some Structures in the Dalradian Pillow Lavas of the Tayvallich Peninsula, Argyll. *Geol. Mag.*, **101**, 481.
WOODWARD, A. S. 1907. On *Scleromochlus Taylori* from the Trias of Elgin. *Quart. J. Geol. Soc.*, **63**, 140.
WRIGHT, W. B. 1908. The Two Earth-Movements of Colonsay. *Quart. J. Geol. Soc.*, **64**, 297.
—— 1911. On a Pre-Glacial Shoreline in the Western Isles of Scotland. *Geol. Mag.*, **8**, 97.
—— 1914. *The Quaternary Ice Age*. London (2nd Edit. 1937).
—— and PEACH, A. M. 1911. The Neolithic Remains of Colonsay, etc. *Geol. Mag.*, **8**, 164.
WYATT, M. 1956. The Monadhliath adamellite, Inverness-shire. *Proc. Geol. Soc.*, **1537**, 86.
WYLLIE, B. K. N. and SCOTT, A. 1913. The Plutonic Rocks of Garabal Hill. *Geol. Mag.*, **10**, 499.

# ADDITIONAL BIBLIOGRAPHY SINCE 1966

## Compiled by D. L. Ross

ALLAN, W. C. 1970. The Morvern–Cabrach basic intrusion. *Scott. Jnl Geol.*, **6**, 53–72.

ANDERTON, R. 1971. Dalradian palaeocurrents from the Jura Quartzite. *Scott. Jnl Geol.*, **7**, 175–8.

ASHCROFT, W. 1970. Note on the contacts of the Belhelvie igneous intrusion. *Scott. Jnl Geol.*, **6**, 73–74.

ATHERTON, M. P. 1968. The variation in garnet, biotite and chlorite composition in medium grade pelitic rocks from the Dalradian, Scotland with particular reference to the zonation in garnet. *Beitr. Miner. Petrog.*, **18**, 347–371.

―― and EDMUNDS, W. M. 1966. An electron microprobe study of some zoned garnets from metamorphic rocks. *Earth Planet. Sci. Lett.*, **1**, 185–93.

BAILEY, ROY A. 1969. Form of the Glen Coe magma chamber and the main fault-intrusion, Scotland. Vol. Abstr., 80–81, *Int. Ass. Volcanol. Chem. Earth's Interior*, Oxford Univ. Dept. Geol. Mineral. 1969.

BERRIDGE, N. G. 1969. A summary of the mineral resources of the "Crofter Counties" of Scotland, comprising Argyllshire, Caithness, Inverness-shire, Orkney and Shetland, Ross and Cromarty and Sutherland. *Rep. No. 69/5, Inst. geol. Sci.*

―― and IVIMEY-COOK, H. C. 1967. The geology of a Geological Survey borehole at Lossiemouth, Morayshire. *Bull. geol. Surv. Gt Br.*, No. 27, 155–69.

BISSET, C. B. 1934. A Contribution to the Study of Some Granites near Aberdeen. *Trans. Edinb. geol. Soc.*, **XIII**, 72–88.

―― 1934. Some Minor Intrusions in South-Central Aberdeenshire. *Trans. Edinb. geol. Soc.*, **XIII**, 133–47.

BLYTH, F. G. H. 1969. Structures in the Southern Part of the Cabrach Igneous Area, Banffshire. *Proc. Geol. Ass.*, **80**, 63–80.

―― 1969. Structures in the Southern Part of the Cabrach Igneous Area, Banffshire. *Proc. Geol. Ass.*, **80**, 63–79.

BORRADAILE, G. J. 1970. The West Limb of the Loch Awe Syncline and the Associated Cleavage Fan. *Geol. Mag.*, **107**, 459.

―― ROBERTS, J. L. and SCRUTTON, C. T. 1971. Supposed Corals from the Dalradian of Scotland. *Nature: Phys. Sci.*, **229**, 179–81.

BOWES, D. R. 1968. The absolute time scale and the subdivision of Precambrian Rocks in Scotland. *Geol. For. Stockh. Forh.*, **90**, 175–88.

―― and CONVERY, H. J. E. 1966. The composition of some Ben Ledi Grits and its bearing on the origin of albite schists in the south-west Highlands. *Scott. Jnl Geol.*, **2**, 67–75.

―― and WRIGHT, A. E. 1967. The Explosion-breccia Pipes near Kentallen, Scotland and their geological setting. *Trans. Roy. Soc. Edinb.*, **67**, 109–42.

BRIDEN, J. C. 1970. Palaeomagnetic Results from the Arrochar and Garabal Hill—Glen Fyne Igneous Complexes, Scotland. *Geophys. J.R. astr. Soc.*, **21**, No. 5.

BROWN, P. E., MILLER, J. A. and GRASTY, R. L. 1968. Isotopic ages of the late-Caledonian granitic intrusions in the British Isles. *Proc. Yorks. geol. Soc.*, **36**, 251–76.

CHINNER, G. A. 1966. The distribution of pressure and temperature during Dalradian metamorphism. *Proc. geol. Soc. Lond.*, No. 1630, 35–6.

―― 1967. Chloritoid and the Isochemical Character of Barrow's Zones. *Jnl Petrology*, **8**, No. 2, 268–87.

DALZIEL, I. W. D. 1968. Tectonic control of Migmatization in the Scottish Caledonides. (Abstr.). *Geol. Soc. Amer. Spec. Pap.*, No. 115, 41–2.

DEWEY, J. F. 1971. A model for the Lower Palaeozoic evolution of the southern margin of the early Caledonides of Scotland and Ireland. *Scott. Jnl Geol.*, **7**, 219–40.

―― and PANKHURST, R. J. 1970. The evolution of the Scottish Caledonides in relation to their isotopic age pattern. *Trans. Roy. Soc. Edinb.*, **63**, 361–89.

DONNER, J. J. 1970. Land/sea level changes in Scotland. In *Studies in the Vegetational History of the British Isles*, 23–39. Cambridge Univ. Press.

EDEN, R. A., SMALL, ANNE V. F. and McQUILLIN, R. 1970. Preliminary report on marine geological and geophysical work off the east coast of Scotland. *Rep. No. 70/1, Inst. geol. Sci.*

FERGUSON, DAVID K. 1966. The structure of the Queen's Cairn Rhyolite, Glen Coe, Argyllshire. *Scott. Jnl Geol.*, **2**, 153–58.

FETTES, D. J. 1970. The structural and metamorphic state of the Dalradian rocks and their bearing on the age of emplacement of the basic sheet. *Scott. Jnl Geol.*, 108–18.

―― 1971. Relation of Cleavage and Metamorphism in the Macduff Slates. *Scott. Jnl Geol.*, **7**, 348–53.

FRIEND, P. F., HARLAND, W. B. and SMITH, A. GILBERT. 1969. Reddening and fissuring associated with the Caledonian unconformity in north-west Arran. (Abstr). *Geol. Ass. (Lond.)* [Circ.], No. 717, 2.

—— and MACDONALD, R. 1968. Volcanic sediments, stratigraphy and tectonic background of the Old Red Sandstone of Kintyre, W. Scotland. *Scott. Jnl Geol.*, 4, 265–82.

GRIBBLE, C. D. 1966. The Thermal Aureole of the Haddo House Norite in Aberdeenshire. *Scott. Jnl Geol.*, 2, 306–13.

—— 1967. The basic intrusive rocks of Caledonian age of the Haddo House and Arnage districts, Aberdeenshire. *Scott. Jnl Geol.*, 3, 135–36.

—— 1968. The cordierite-bearing rocks of the Haddo House and Arnage districts, Aberdeenshire. *Contrib. Mineral. Petrology-Beitr. Mineral. Petrologie*, 17, 315–30.

—— 1970. The role of partial fusion in the genesis of certain cordierite-bearing rocks, *Scott. Jnl Geol.*, 6, 75–82.

HALL, A. 1969. Regional variation in the composition of Caledonian granitic rocks. *Proc. geol. Soc. Lond.*, No. 1654, 51–4.

HARDIE, W. G. 1968. Volcanic breccia and the Lower Old Red Sandstone unconformity, Glen Coe, Argyll. *Scott. Jnl Geol.*, 4, 291–99.

HARPER, C. T. 1967. The geological interpretation of potassium-argon ages of metamorphic rocks from the Scottish Caledonides. *Scott. Jnl Geol.*, 3, 46–66.

—— 1970. Graphical solutions to the problem of radiogenic argon-40 loss from metamorphic minerals. *Eclog. geol. Helv.*, 63, 119–40. (Data from Caledonides of Scotland and Ireland.)

HARRIS, A. L. 1969. The relationships of the Leny Limestone to the Dalradian. *Scott. Jnl Geol.*, 5, 187–90.

—— and BERRIDGE, N. G. 1969. The geology of the Nant hydro-electric tunnels. *Bull. geol. Surv. Gt Br.*, No. 30, 99–114.

—— and PEACOCK, J. D. 1969. Sand and gravel resources of the Inner Moray Firth. *Rep. No. 69/9, Inst. geol. Sci.*

HARTE, B. and JOHNSON, M. R. W. 1969. Metamorphic history of Dalradian rocks in Glens Clova, Esk and Lethnot, Angus, Scotland. *Scott. Jnl Geol.*, 5, 81–9.

HASLAM, H. W. 1968. The Crystallization of Intermediate and Acid Magmas at Ben Nevis, Scotland. *Jnl Petrology*, 9, No. 1.

—— 1970. Appinite xenoliths and associated rocks from the Ben Nevis igneous complex. *Geol. Mag.*, 107, 341.

HAYNES, VALERIE M. 1968. The influence of glacial erosion and rock structures on corries in Scotland. *Geogr. Ann.*, Ser. A, 50, 221–34.

HOLGATE, N. 1969. Palaeozoic and Tertiary transcurrent movements on the Great Glen Fault. *Scott. Jnl Geol.*, 5, 97–139.

JARDINE, W. G. 1968. Letters to the Editor, "The 'Perth' Readvance". *Scott. Jnl Geol.*, 4, 185.

JOHNSTONE, G. S. and CRICHTON, J. R. 1966. Geological and civil engineering aspects of hydroelectric developments in the Scottish Highlands. *Engng Geol.*, 1, 311–42.

JOHNSON, M. R. W. and HARRIS, A. L. 1967. Dalradian–Arenig relations in parts of the Highland Border, Scotland, and their significance in the chronology of the Caledonian orogeny. *Scott. Jnl Geol.*, 3, 1–16.

KING, R. B. 1971. Boulder polygons and stripes in the Cairngorm Mountains, Scotland. *Jnl Glaciol.*, 10, No. 60.

KLEIN, GEORGE DE VRIES. 1970. Tidal Origin of a Precambrian Quartzite—the Lower Fine-Grained Quartzite (Middle Dalradian) of Islay, Scotland. *Jnl sedim. Petrol.*, 40, 973–85.

MATHER, J. D. 1970. The Biotite Isograd and the Lower Greenschist Facies in the Dalradian rocks of Scotland. (Aberfoyle area). *Jnl Petrology*, 11, 254–76.

MARSTON, R. J. 1967. Newer Granites of Foyers and Strontian and the Great Glen Fault. *Nature, Lond.*, 214, 159–61.

McCANN, S. B. 1966. The limits of the Late-glacial Highland, or Loch Lomond, Readvance along the West Highland seaboard from Oban to Mallaig. *Scott. Jnl Geol.*, 2, 84–95.

MILES, ROGER S. and WESTOLL, T. STANLEY. 1968. The Placoderm Fish *Coccosteus cuspidatus* Miller ex Agassiz from the Middle Old Red Sandstone of Scotland; Part 1, Descriptive Morphology. *Trans. Roy. Soc. Edinb.*, 67, 373–474.

MUNRO, M. 1970. A re-assessment of the "younger" basic igneous rocks between Huntley and Portsoy. *Scott. Jnl Geol.*, 6, 41–52.

O'HARA, M. J. and STEWART, F. H. 1966. Olivine-Liquid Reaction and the Depth of Crystallization of the East Aberdeenshire Gabbros. *Nature, Lond.*, 210, 830–31.

PANKHURST, R. J. 1969. Strontium isotope studies applied to petrogenesis in the basic igneous province of N.E. Scotland. *Jnl Petrology*, 10, 116–45.

—— 1970. The geochronology of the basic igneous complexes. *Scott. Jnl Geol.*, 6, 83–107.

PATERSON, I. B. and HARRIS, A. L. 1969. Lower Old Red Sandstone ignimbrites from Dunkeld, Perthshire. *Rep. No.* 69/7, *Inst. geol. Sci.*

PATZAK, ALOIS and SHEPHARD, ELIZABETH. 1969. Im mittelschottischen Hoghland; I die Naturlandschaft von Aberfeldy, Crianlarich und die Moors of Rannoch, und das Ben Laaers-Gebiet [The central Scottish Highlands; 1, The natural Landscape of Aberfeldy, Crianlarich and the Rannoch Moors and the Ben Lawers area]. *Osterreich Geogr. Ges., Mitt.*, 111, 67–72.

PEACOCK, J. D. 1966. Note on the drift sequence near Portsoy, Banffshire. *Scott. Jnl Geol.*, 2, 35–7.

—— 1966. Contorted beds in the Permo-Triassic aeolian sandstones of Morayshire. *Bull. geol. Surv. Gt Br.*, No. 24, 157–62.

—— 1971. Marine Shell Radiocarbon Dates and the Chronology of Deglaciation in Western Scotland. *Nature: Phys. Sci.*, 230, 43–5.

QURESHI, I. R. 1970. A gravity survey of a region of the Highland Boundary Fault in Scotland. *Q. Jnl geol. Soc. Lond.*, 125, 481–502.

RAST, N. and LITHERLAND, M. 1970. The correlation of the Ballachulish and Perthshire (Iltay) Dalradian successions. *Geol. Mag.*, 107, 259.

ROBERTS, J. L. 1966. Sedimentary affiliations and stratigraphic correlation of the Dalradian rocks in the South-west Highlands of Scotland. *Scott. Jnl Geol.*, 2, 200–23.

—— 1966. The Emplacement of the Main Glencoe Fault-Intrusion at Stob Mhic Mhartuin. *Geol. Mag.*, 103, 299–316.

SABINE, P. A. and WATSON, JANET V. 1967. Isotopic age-determinations of rocks and minerals from the British Isles, 1965; with an introduction. *Q. Jnl geol. Soc. Lond.*, 122, 443–60.

SIMPSON, A. 1968. The Caledonian history of the north-eastern Irish Sea region and its relation to surrounding areas. *Scott. Jnl Geol.*, 4, 135–63.

SISSONS, J. B. 1967. *The Evolution of Scotland's Scenery*. Hamden: Connecticut.

—— 1968. The "Perth" readvance. [Discussion]. *Scott. Jnl Geol.*, 4, 186–87.

SKEVINGTON, D. 1971. Palaeontological evidence bearing on the age of Dalradian deformation and metamorphism in Ireland and Scotland. *Scott. Jnl Geol.*, 7, 285–88.

—— and STURT, B. A. 1967. Faunal Evidence bearing on the Age of Late Cambrian–Early Ordovician Metamorphism in Britain and Norway. *Nature, Lond.*, 215, 608–9.

SMITH, D. G. W. 1969. Pyrometamorphism of Phyllites by a Dolerite Plug (Strachur, Loch Fyne—Argyllshire). *Jnl Petrology.*, 10, 20–53.

SMITH, T. E. 1968. Tectonics in Upper Strathspey, Inverness-shire. *Scott. Jnl Geol.*, 4, 68–84.

—— 1970. The structural characteristics of the Strathspey Complex, Inverness-shire. *Geol. Mag.*, 107, 201.

SPENCER, A. M. 1969. Late Pre-Cambrian Glaciation in Scotland. *Proc. geol. Soc. Lond.*, No. 1657. 177–98.

—— 1971. Late Pre-Cambrian Glaciation in Scotland (Port Askaig–Dalradian). *Mem. geol. Soc. Lond.*, No. 6.

—— and PITCHER, W. S. 1968. Occurrence of the Port Askaig Tillite in north-east Scotland. *Proc. geol. Soc. Lond.*, No. 1650.

STEWART, F. H. 1970. Introduction (to "The 'younger' basic igneous complexes of northeast Scotland, and their metamorphic envelope"). *Scott. Jnl Geol.*, 6, 3–6.

SUGDEN, D. E. 1968. The selectivity of glacial erosion in the Cairngorm Mountains, Scotland. *Trans. Inst. Br. Geogr.*, 45, 79–92.

—— 1969. The Age and Form of Corries in the Cairngorms. *Scott. geogr. Mag.*, 85, 34–46.

SUMMERHAYES, C. P. 1966. A Geochronological and Strontium Isotope Study on the Garabal Hill–Glen Fyne Igneous Complex, Scotland. *Geol. Mag.*, 103, 153–65.

SUTTON, J. 1967. The extension of the geological record into the Pre-Cambrian. *Proc. Geol. Ass.*, 78, 493–534.

TAUBENECK, W. H. 1967. Notes on the Glen Coe Cauldron Subsidence, Argyllshire. *Geol. Soc. Amer. Bull.*, 78.

THOMAS, P. R. and TREAGUS, J. E. 1968. The Stratigraphy and Structure of the Glen Orchy Area, Argyllshire, Scotland. *Scott. Jnl Geol.*, 4, 121–34.

TREAGUS, J. E. 1969. The Kinlochlaggan Boulder Bed. *Proc. geol. Soc. Lond.*, No. 1654, 55–60.

—— 1969. The Kinlochlaggan Boulder Bed. [Discussion]. *Proc. geol. Soc. Lond.*, No. 1657, 198.

—— and TREAGUS, S. H. 1971. The structures of the Ardsheal Peninsula, Argyll, their age and regional significance. *Lpool Manchr geol. Jnl*, 7, 335–46.

VAN DE KAMP, P. C. 1970. The Green Beds of the Scottish Dalradian Series: Geochemistry, Origin, and Metamorphism of Mafic Sediments. *Jnl Geol.*, 78, 281–303.

WADSWORTH, W. J. 1970. The Aberdeenshire Layered Intrusion of North-East Scotland in Bushveld Igneous Complex and other Layered Intrusions. Symposium. *Geol. Soc. S. Afr., Spec. Publ.*, No. 1.
—— STEWART, F. H. and ROTHSTEIN, A. T. V. 1966. Cryptic layering in the Belhelvie intrusion, Aberdeenshire. *Scott. Jnl Geol.*, **2,** 54–66.
WEEDON, D. S. 1970. The ultrabasic/basic igneous rocks of the Huntly region. *Scott. Jnl Geol.*, **6,** 26–40.
WESTOLL, N. D. S. and MILLER, J. A. 1969. The ages of some kentallenite intrusions in Argyll. *Scott. Jnl Geol.*, **5,** 11–4.
WILSON, C. D. V. 1970. Geophysical studies of the basic intrusions. *Scott. Jnl Geol.*, **6,** 119–25.
—— and RAST, N. 1969. Old Red Sandstone of Kintyre. *Scott. Jnl Geol.*, **5,** 90–4.
WILSON, M. J. 1967. The clay mineralogy of some soils derived from a biotite-rich quartz-gabbro in the Strathdon area, Aberdeenshire. *Clay Miner.*, **7,** 91–100.
—— BERROW, M. L. and MCHARDY, W. J. 1970. Lithiophorite from the Lecht Mines, Tomintoul, Banffshire. *Mineralog. Mag.*, **37,** No. 289, 618–23.
ZIEGLER, A. M. 1970. Geosynclinal Development of the British Isles during the Silurian period. *Jnl Geol.*, **78,** 445–79.

Printed in Scotland for Her Majesty's Stationery Office
by Hugh K. Clarkson & Sons Ltd., West Calder,
Cover and Art Section by Bell & Bain Ltd., Glasgow. Dd.020010 K 48.